Unwin Education Books: 14

READING AND WRITING IN THE FIRST SCHOOL

Unwin Education Books

Series Editor: Ivor Morrish, B.D., B.A., Dip. Ed. (London), B.A. (Bristol)

Unwin Education Books: 14
Series Editor: Ivor Morrish

Reading and Writing in the First School

JOY TAYLOR
M.A. (Hons)
Head of Education Department
The Lady Spencer-Churchill College of Education, Wheatley, Oxford

London
GEORGE ALLEN AND UNWIN LTD
RUSKIN HOUSE MUSEUM STREET

First published in 1973
Second impression 1974

ISBN 0 04 372005 6 hardback
     0 04 372006 4 paperback

Printed in Great Britain
in 11 point Times Roman
by Clarke, Doble & Brendon Ltd, Plymouth

To Iris and Angus Urquhart
whose respect for education laid
the foundations of this book

Acknowledgements

I am greatly indebted to Miss Joan Webb, the Librarian at the Lady Spencer-Churchill College of Education, and to her assistant Miss Lorraine Kent, who went to considerable trouble to obtain for me some of the books and journals I have used; to Mrs Betty Carter who very kindly typed the manuscript; and to the many writers and researchers upon whose work I have drawn in assembling my material.

Preface

This book does not set out to add anything new to theoretical knowledge about the teaching of reading and writing; the reader who looks for significant and dramatically revealing answers to the questions of how to teach these skills to young children will be disappointed. There are a great many books and studies, especially on reading, and it is in these that the teacher will find the detail and the depth that strengthen her professional expertise.

There does, however, seem to be a need for a practical exposition of the subject, which marries the main trends of the theory to the practice and which provides a springboard for the further study in depth that must be acknowledged as essential to the effective teacher. The student and those who are still inexperienced may, in particular, find that such a spring-board gives them a workable starting point. It is for them that this book is primarily designed, and the author is much indebted to all the researchers and writers upon whose material most of us depend for our theoretical understanding of the ways in which we teach.

There is a danger inherent in the somewhat global approach of this book. It is the danger of superficiality. The teaching of reading and writing is such an extensive subject that the problems of the selection of material and of its presentation in a concise and practical form are acute. These problems have not, in fact, been wholly solved, nor is a charge of superficiality quite without foundation. Nevertheless, in order that the teacher may decide upon the 'how' of teaching, she must have a working knowledge of the 'why'—and she must then unite them into the 'what'. The advantages of a combined approach in one volume may perhaps counteract the disadvantages which arise from the fact that so much has to be omitted. Extensive references for further reading are given in the text, and the bibliography lists titles which will reward the teacher who is really concerned to know her subject. It may be that an introduction such as this book provides will make the task a little easier for the reader who, early in her career, recognises the need to learn more.

J.M.T.

Contents

Chapter 1

Learning and Teaching

Giving evidence before a Parliamentary Committee appointed to investigate the State of Education in 1834, a witness was asked: 'If a man were sufficiently well skilled in writing, reading and arithmetic, he could learn in five months the difficult art of teaching?' The witness was in no doubt. 'Yes, decidedly; and it may be learnt in three months, if he has tact. . . .'

With our more sophisticated understanding of learning and teaching we have added considerably to the rudimentary requirement of our forbears. The modern teacher, particularly at the outset of her career, may be forgiven if even after three or four years' training there are times when her tact seems unlikely to hold out. Teachers today know that their 'training' will continue throughout their teaching lives; and this continued training must be acquired while meeting the demands which any full-time job presents, and in the face of a mounting accumulation of literature to be assimilated and applied. The purpose of this book is to try to make this process a little easier for the busy, and particularly the inexperienced, teacher —to gather together the main threads of the theory which is emerging, and to relate it to the practice as constructively and as realistically as possible.

There has, and rightly, long been a reaction against the rigours and the limitations of very formal teaching. However, one now detects a growing unease at the widespread implication that to *teach* a child to read and write at all is not only unnecessary, it is downright reprehensible. In its extreme form this view inclines to the belief that all the teacher must do is provide an environment in which the children are set free to satisfy their unquenchable thirst for knowledge, and most of them will, with little difficulty, 'discover' it all for themselves.

There is no longer any need to emphasise the value of the child's freedom in the modern classroom to investigate, to experiment, to absorb, to learn by living in a learning environment. But within this environment there are some areas of learning which the teacher must present in a logical, carefully formulated progression, each step for the child following upon a proper understanding of the one before. Reading and writing are among the areas of learning which come unequivocally into this category. There are some materials and activities and experiences which are appropriate to a particular child at any given time; and there are others which are not. It is the teacher's responsibility, not the child's, to make the selection.

Only the very gifted and the very privileged child is likely to learn to read and write without very deliberate measures being taken by the teacher to enable him to do so. Let us then accept that for all the rest *teaching* is crucial. As far as reading, at any rate, is concerned this is not a subjective view. It is supported in a research study carried out by Dr Joyce Morris and reported in *Standards and Progress in Reading*, published by the National Foundation for Educational Research in 1966. And in her introduction to *The Teaching of Reading* by Donald Moyle Dr Morris refers to his central theme :

We are reminded that reading is a product of civilisation not, like physical growth, a natural phenomenon. Hence, children generally will neither begin to learn to read nor proceed to acquire the necessary reading skills if left to their own devices no matter how rich the reading environment provided by their teachers. They must be given systematic instruction based on an accurate diagnosis of their individual needs throughout their school lives.[1]

In learning to write, the young child is setting out to master a skill, or, more accurately, a range of skills, which are far from easy. To begin with, he must learn to control a pencil, and then he must learn to form the actual shapes and patterns of the written language and to assemble them in certain recognisable word units. Some children experience real difficulty in doing just this. But the task is only just begun. A specialist in linguistics clearly describes the learning that lies ahead :

[1] Donald Moyle, *The Teaching of Reading*, 2nd edn (London, Ward Lock Educational, 1970), p. 9.

It is when children have to pass from the imitative to the creative aspect of writing that the real troubles begin. Here they are being faced with a task that demands an integration of much more complex skills. They have not only to think out clearly what they intend to write—and this is difficult enough for many of them—but, in addition, to organise these thoughts on paper, to manipulate language in what is a comparatively unfamiliar form, and—the crucial test—to do this in such a way as to make themselves understood by the reader.[2]

Add to this the development of the child's imagination and his powers of creative thought so that his writing may give him pleasure and purpose and we have some idea of all that learning to write involves.

Surely there can be no real doubt that there is a case for actually teaching children to read and write. The teacher, conscious of her objectives, must devise the means by which she hopes to achieve them. If she accepts that there is a progression, she must know what it is; and she must then break down the whole into manageable parts which each child can engage in at his own pace and in accordance with his own individual needs. The child must, above all, have some chance of success with each of these separate parts, or his learning and his progress will suffer quite seriously.

He will not be successful if he is not interested and this is where a rich and stimulating environment, and an organisation which actively encourages him to make his personal effort, are so vital. But the environment and the organisation do no more than provide the essential setting. The teacher, in partnership with the child, must make use of the setting in such a way that the child will learn.

It is only too easy to make it sound as though, given the setting and the teaching, every child will learn to read and write without difficulty. This, of course, is neither true nor realistic, as every practitioner knows. It does not, however, invalidate the plea made here for the teaching of reading and writing to take place within the environment and not be ex-

[2] Hugh Fraser, 'The Teaching of Writing', in H. Fraser and W. R. O'Donnell (eds), *Applied Linguistics and the Teaching of English* (London, Longman, 1969), p. 123.

cluded from it as though it were superfluous in a really up-to-date approach. The development of the personal autonomy of the child and his active participation in learning situations all around him need never be in conflict with the teacher's responsibility to teach him the basic skills and to encourage their development as far as the child can go.

It is on the basis of this conviction that an attempt will be made in the following chapters to review some of the theoretical foundations which support the teaching of reading and writing; to examine ways in which such teaching may be approached; to delineate the stages of progression in reading and writing as they apply to children in their early years in school; and to offer a variety of practical suggestions which reflect this progression and which the teacher may adapt to the circumstances and needs of the children she is teaching.

In order to present the practical aspect as clearly as possible, the progression in reading is broken down into four stages which more or less span the First School years. These stages are not specifically related to age, but rather to levels of development which will be reached by some children more quickly than by others. A few may indeed be beyond the first stage at the age of five, while some, of course, will not complete all four stages before the end of the First School. There will clearly be a range of achievement within each stage as the children learn and mature and as their reading advances. The four stages will be described as:

(i) *The pre-readers.* These are the children who have not yet begun to interpret the printed word at all and may need a good deal of preparation before they can do so. Clearly most of them will also, to begin with at any rate, be the youngest.

(ii) *The beginners.* These children are just at the point when reading is beginning to mean something. They may recognise a few words, provided they meet them in a familiar context. They are just moving towards reading, though it cannot be said that they are yet readers.

(iii) *The advancing readers.* They have begun. 'Reading' is no longer a mysterious art which people talk about, but a skill which is real and recognisable and these children know they are learning to acquire it. They can read a respectable total of words, but many of these words only in a context in which they expect to meet them. Where reading is to be used for some particular purpose, such as following the instruction on an assignment card, a fairly carefully controlled vocabulary is still necessary.

(iv) *The fluent readers.* These children can read; that is to say, they can interpret, without experiencing any major technical difficulty, virtually all they encounter in print. Their need now is to develop their reading skill and use it for personal satisfaction and enlightenment, and as a tool for the extension of their learning in a great range of activity and interest that is now open to them.

Some children do not progress through any, or all, of these levels of development without a great deal of extra help and without special measures being taken to help them to overcome the difficulties they experience in learning to read. Indeed, some of them may not be nearly as successful with their reading as we should like during their First School years. There are, however, steps which the teacher can take to help such children, and if she can even loosen the log which is jamming the pile she may be doing a great deal towards moderating the child's sense of failure. A chapter is included on remedial measures which may be appropriate in such cases.

A child's ability to write does not necessarily correspond with his ability to read. A really good reader, whose intellectual equipment may be considerable, may yet experience quite exceptional difficulty in committing pencil to paper. Conversely there are children who can, without undue effort, master the physical skill of forming letters and words, but who are unable either to read the words they have written or to put their skill to use as an interpretative or communicative tool.

The first stage of learning to master the art of handwriting may therefore apply to a child in any of the four suggested stages of learning to read; and the teacher will bear this in mind when considering the writing stages. Despite this reservation, however, there is a certain progression in learning to write, assuming that writing is taken to mean much more than mere proficiency in a comparatively low level skill.

The fact that writing helps reading and reading stimulates writing makes it somewhat artificial, in practice, to try to separate the two activities. Teaching the child to write will therefore be dealt with alongside teaching the child to read, on the assumption that the teacher's detailed demand on each child is modified or extended according to his personal capacity.

In teaching children to read and write, there is much that we still do not know with any degree of certainty. We clearly must give serious thought to that which is known and to that which is indicated by the evidence at present available. But, for the rest, we are still acting on observation, on common sense, on experience, and individually on the methods which seem to bear fruit. Some children undoubtedly appear to learn better with this kind of material, others react more favourably to that. No book on the teaching of reading and writing can claim to describe the perfect method which will suit every teacher and every child. A variety of approach is surely essential if individual needs are to be reasonably well satisfied. It is only the teacher, in a very particular situation, who can decide upon the right 'mix' for Mark, and Susan, and Janet. The most that any book can hope to do is to suggest which ingredients are available for the mix and to indicate why these particular ingredients are on the market. The teacher, ultimately, must make the decision as to the proportions which suit her children best.

Chapter 2

Learning to Read—Some Basic Issues

A great deal of time and thought has been given, over many years, to the question of trying to establish with some precision the mental processes by which children learn to read. It would be far from accurate to imply that teachers and researchers are still no nearer to identifying any convincing lines of advance than they were in the days before it was fashionable to give so much attention to the teaching of reading. There is now, for example, quite an impressive accumulation of evidence which suggests that children can be helped to look at the component parts of words and find clues that help them in word recognition. This is an extremely important hypothesis, in terms of practical teaching, which seriously undermines the validity of the wholly 'look-and-say' approach that not so long ago was almost exclusively advocated—at least until children were considered to be sufficiently mature to dissect words or even sentences into smaller parts.

On the other hand evidence concerning cognitive processes, however carefully assembled, inevitably depends to some extent upon subjective interpretation; and in any case there is still much that is not conclusively known. There is more than one theory of how children learn, and certainly more than one view of the mechanisms by which they learn to read. The teacher must therefore weigh up the evidence available and the interpretations put upon it, and then determine upon a course of action which, it is hoped, will yield results. We obviously cannot wait to teach children to read until we are certain beyond doubt of the best way of doing so.

We must, however, try to take account of the probability

that not all children may learn by precisely the same procedures. If teachers are to do this, they need to know something of current opinion concerning these learning procedures. They are then in a better position to allow, as far as in practice they can, for more than one possible way of learning. This assumption obviously cannot be carried too far. There are limits to the permutations which any presentation of material or fluidity of class organisation will permit, and in any case the teacher who is caused to worry so much about all the things she may not be doing could well be inhibited from being effective in the practice she already employs to some purpose. Nevertheless, familiarity with current opinion may enable her to extend the possibilities of learning within the practical framework of the conditions of her class.

LEARNING THEORIES

One theory is that learning is a process of conditioning. (The dog that learns to come for food when he hears his dinner bowl being rattled is responding to this principle.) By associating, for example, the word 'cat' with a picture of a cat, the child will in time be conditioned to making the association even when he sees the word without the picture. Taken a little further, the child is more likely to respond effectively to the conditioning if the material with which he is concerned has interest for him and is related to his daily life. On this assumption, it may be more likely that the child will be 'conditioned' to learn to read 'dog' because his Fido is a dog than to read 'jackal' since he does not ordinarily meet jackals as he walks down the road.

Reinforcement is an essential part of conditioning. A single experience of associating word and picture is unlikely to be enough. Repeated association is necessary (with more repetition for some children than for others); and since interest must be sustained a variety of ways in which identical word and picture situations can be presented must be devised. It is also important to recognise that conditioning will not be equally effective with every child.

The normal provision in an infant classroom will usually include material of this kind. Modern reading theory, how-

ever, suggests that there is more to it than straightforward whole word/picture association—that the child certainly seems to use more detailed clues to help his memory. (This will be further discussed later in the chapter.) It must be remembered, too, that words and pictures are not the only associations that provide for conditioning. Letter/sound associations may be made in the same way and so indeed may many others. It is the *principle* of conditioning that has theoretical significance for the teacher.

Another theory, primarily associated with the work of Piaget, is that learning is cumulative. It builds upon, and incorporates, past experience. A child's response to a particular situation will bring about certain results. The next time he meets a similar situation, he will meet it with certain expectations which arise as a consequence of his earlier experience—in other words, he learns to anticipate the result of his actions in known circumstances. The child assimilates the consequences of his experience as it accumulates, and in due course he *internalises* his actions and they become thoughts. He can then organise these thoughts so that he can adapt them in order to learn from the next situation.

In his earlier writings Piaget suggested that this process of adaptation operates more readily and with greater versatility as the child matures and develops. Indeed, he implied that at the beginning of the First School years most children are at the stage when, in effect, they believe the evidence of their eyes— their mental assumptions are largely based on imagery. They do not have the power of interpreting differences they see by making intellectual deductions; that is to say, they may distinguish a long word from a short one when they meet it in a known context, but they distinguish it because it is clearly long and not for any reason which has been intellectually deduced.

At a later stage of intellectual maturity, the child would be able to use his experience of seeing and hearing words to abstract certain characteristics which were not entirely dependent upon imagery. For example, he could deduce that 'hop' becomes 'hope' because of the addition of the terminal 'e'. This hypothesis can hardly be at variance with the experience of the teacher of children who are learning to read. We all

know that there is no point in talking about the 'magic e' to the child who has not made a start with even simple word recognition. The significance of the developmental theory, however, is the implication that progress is, in essence, a function of maturation. In recent years more weight has been attached to the view that *training* may play a greater part in precipitating learning than Piaget originally implied.

In practical terms, the developmental theory would lead the teacher to concentrate on giving the child as rich and varied an experience as possible in all the activities and materials which may help him to learn to read. She may also try to 'precipitate' his learning by helping him to make intellectual deductions which, without her positive help, might be unduly delayed.

All this would mean plenty of opportunity to use language, to see and compare word—and possibly letter—shapes (i.e. matching), to associate visual and auditory patterns and to perceive the mental connection between what the child hears described as 'reading' and the printed patterns he sees in the books and other materials which he handles; and the teacher provides for learning of this kind with the environment she establishes, the materials and activities she makes available, and the teaching which helps the child to move through a logical reading progression.

A third theory which may have an important bearing on learning to read is concerned with learning by 'insight'. When faced with a learning situation the child, on the basis of his knowledge existing at that time, considers for himself the nature of the problem and tries to find its solution. It would seem that there may be an element of trial and error before the solution is found, and the child may, for a number of reasons, jump to inaccurate conclusions before he comes to the right one. For example, in trying to read 'little' he may at first say 'kitten' because of the 'tt' in both words. He finds, perhaps by being told, perhaps from a piece of self-correcting apparatus, that the word is not 'kitten'. On a subsequent occasion, slight modification of his earlier insight may enable him to arrive at the new correct solution.

Lovell suggests that almost all children have some degree of insight, even though they may be dull. '. . . insightful be-

haviour is possible at all levels of intelligence in children, provided the learning task is at the correct level of difficulty. On this view, the task of the teacher is to start from whatever insight his pupils possess and to direct them to new situations of the appropriate complexity which they can solve by insight.'[1]

A range of matching activities (some of which might be self-correcting) would help the child who may learn in this way, as would those of the 'put a ring round the right word' variety, selecting the correct sound to attach to the beginning or end of the word, and other material of this nature. Since the success of insight learning depends to some extent on the insights a child already possesses, he would seem more likely to profit from it once he has made a beginning in recognising what reading means; but when this point comes, it is unlikely that special provision will be necessary. Materials which would help the child are generally to be found in most infant classrooms.

THE PROCESS OF LEARNING TO READ

Having considered briefly three of the learning theories which may be directly applicable to reading, we should now examine in more detail how the actual process of learning to read is thought to take place.

This learning undoubtedly calls upon a considerable range of abilities and skills, both innate and acquired, and there are in addition other factors (for example temperament) which appear to make a significant contribution. No useful attempt can be made to arrange all these elements in order of importance, partly because we do not know enough about it to establish such an order, and partly because some elements are likely to be more important than others according to individual differences in children. We do, however, need to be aware of what these elements are believed to be, and we should try to consider them directly in relation to classroom practice as far as it is possible to do this realistically in a book.

[1] K. Lovell, *Educational Psychology and Children*, 5th edn (London, University of London Press, 1962), p. 116.

EYE MOVEMENT AND FIXATION SPAN

It is known that in reading, the eye (in our written language) travels from left to right in a series of movements and momentary pauses. It is during the pauses, often known as *fixations*, that reading takes place. Schonell explains that 'during each eye pause the [skilled] reader fully recognises two or three words in the material being read, and partially recognises a word or two on either side. The amount properly recognised at one pause is called the *span of recognition* . . .'[2] (also called the *fixation span*).

The size of the fixation span is dependent upon the skill of the reader and the difficulty of the material. The beginner may well assimilate only two or three letters in one fixation. The fluent reader probably makes good use of the areas of partial recognition to comprehend what is being read and to anticipate the next words, but the extent to which the child just beginning to read can make use of this assistance is doubtful. In his concentration on 'decoding' he tends to forget what he has already seen and so his eyes must repeatedly move back to re-register the earlier impression. It is therefore most important that the difficulty of the material should be matched to the child. Too many eye movements (particularly those which are regressive) will retard fluency and comprehension. The teacher's contribution here is to try to ensure that the reading material presented to the child is progressively graded so that it may lead him on and not hold him back.

We tend to assume that children will naturally move their eyes from left to right when learning to read, but Goodacre found that this is not necessarily so.[3] The teacher may well need to help the child to form this habit. She could run her finger unobtrusively along the word or phrase the child is trying to read, casually draw his attention to the direction in which she is writing for him while he watches, and help him to start at the left when he begins to write or trace his own name. It is doubtful whether this help would be necessary for long

[2] Fred J. Schonell, *The Psychology and Teaching of Reading*, 4th edn (Edinburgh, Oliver & Boyd, 1961), p. 33.
[3] Elizabeth J. Goodacre, *Children and Learning to Read* (London, Routledge & Kegan Paul, 1971), p. 6.

and once the habit is formed the child is unlikely to try to reverse it.

UNIT OF RECOGNITION

There has long been some diversity of view as to whether the unit which children begin by recognising most easily is the letter, the word, or the phrase or 'sentence'. Schonell was emphatic that the child responds primarily 'to the total visual pattern of the whole word . . . it is the marked differences in the visual patterns of the words as wholes which enable him to recognise each word'.[4] He stressed the importance of differences in length and of variations in shape caused by projecting letters. Hence the vogue among teachers for some time of outlining words in order to draw the child's attention to these differences in visual patterns, for example

come   look

Despite his emphasis on the visual pattern of the whole word, however, Schonell did not exclude the child's use of other clues in word recognition. He noted the use of initial and final letters as clues, of known syllables, of double letters and of meaning. 'It would seem,' he said, 'that recognition of a word is based on a combination of the total shape of a word, of groups of letters (as in the double 't' in 'little') and of individual letters in it.'[5]

Schonell's *Happy Venture* reading scheme was published in 1937. Later a determined movement towards being concerned with the 'whole child' developed. This resulted for a time in the widespread acceptance of the view that learning to read was a natural part of the child's total development; and that as long as the learning environment encouraged this, he would learn to read by a kind of 'absorption' process in which attention to detailed reading skills was out of place. This view is crystallised by Mellor: '. . . children will learn to

[4] Schonell, op. cit., p. 11.
[5] Schonell, ibid., p. 14.

read by listening and reading, as they learnt to talk by listening and talking.'[6]

The happy long-term result of this climate of opinion has been to give far greater attention to the variety of influences which affect a child's ability to learn, and to try to eliminate unnecessary conventions which inhibit or constrict. But the less fortunate effects were that the teacher was too often diverted from an examination of detailed learning processes, and in teaching reading she was sometimes led to an almost exclusive concern with 'meaning' and 'fluency'. She was given to understand that anything more specific must inevitably result in 'barking at print'.

Teaching which directed attention to letters or individual sounds or even, at its extreme, to just one word, was therefore frowned upon. The sentence method, which admirably fitted this global view in its lack of concern with detail, was widely used. It was not easy, however, to escape the controlled vocabulary if the thing was to be kept within bounds. The result was a spate of reading schemes described by Dr Margaret Peters as 'both boring and far removed from children's own idiom. . . . As vehicles of "meaning" they were a complete failure; as stimulants to literacy, they were disastrous.'[7]

In the meantime, however, serious attention was again being given to trying to establish whether the unit of recognition to which the child was most likely to respond was not in fact something much more detailed than the phrase or sentence—or, indeed, than the whole word. It began to be whispered abroad that children *do* look at letter shapes, particularly those at the beginning and end of words, and at times appear to use them as clues.

This question of the clues which children seem to use to help them in word recognition has, in recent years, been much considered. There is growing evidence to support the view that the unit of recognition *is* the whole word but that letter shapes and sounds are among the most significant clues which help children to distinguish one word from another.

Daniels and Diack developed this theory in England and

[6] E. Mellor, *Education Through Experience in the Infant School Years* (Oxford, Blackwell, 1950), p. 136.

[7] Margaret L. Peters, *Trends in Reading Schemes* (Cambridge, University Institute of Education pamphlet, 1971), p. 3.

presented it in practical form in the *Royal Road Readers* published in 1954. They describe their approach as the 'phonic word method'. It differs from the strictly phonic method in that it begins with whole words and identifies the letter differences, both by sight and by sound, in order to distinguish one word from another; whereas the phonic method begins with the sounds of the letters and then fuses or synthesises them to build the word—hence the description of the phonic method as 'synthetic'.

Daniels and Diack are concerned not only with word recognition, but also with word meaning.

The phonic word method . . . whilst not rejecting modern theories of maturation based upon the child's interests and play activities, pays much greater attention to the training of visual perception and the teaching of letters than do methods based upon word-whole theories. The *Royal Road Readers* are based upon a scheme of graded phonics which, however, do not so concentrate on teaching letter meanings that word meanings are neglected. Indeed the main idea which gave the material its shape and design was that, at all times, the child should be looking through letter-meanings to word-meanings. The necessity for going beyond mere 'word recognition', beyond mere 'word-calling' to word-meanings is imposed upon the child by the design of the teaching materials.[8]

In an extensive investigation Daniels and Diack found that both in word recognition and in comprehension children taught by the phonic word method were 'significantly superior' to those taught by mixed methods, in the tests by which their reading was measured.

A variation of this view formulated by Eleanor Gibson and her colleagues (1962) is that it is the letter group or phoneme pattern which is the critical unit of language and to which the child's attention should be drawn when he is learning to read. Roberts interprets this specifically.

Reading is now seen as decoding the phonemic or sound patterns of spoken language rather than decoding single letters . . . these letter/sound correspondences should be in-

[8] J. C. Daniels and Hunter Diack, *Progress in Reading in the Infant School* (Nottingham, University Institute of Education, 1960), pp. 7–8.

troduced in different contexts, so that the child can see them operating in many different words, and thereby learn and understand their invariant relationship. In this way the child will achieve more easily what he has to learn anyhow—to perceive as units the clusters of letters that represent the basic sounds of spoken language.[9]

The significance for the teacher of these developments is that they are founded on evidence which casts serious doubts on the effectiveness of the exclusive use of look-and-say methods, whether these are based on whole word or, perhaps especially, on sentence recognition. The widespread use of the sentence method was based on the belief that since children's thought and their language take place in sentences or phrases, it is logical that they should begin to read in the same way. The child was presented with short sentences associated with a picture, a major advantage being that there need be no restriction on relating the material very much to the learner's everyday life and activities. It was thought that at first the child would 'read' the sentence by memorising it in conjunction with the picture and eventually he would come to recognise the sentence without the help of the picture. In due course, he would isolate words which he could then read in the true sense, and finally he would break down the word into letters and sounds.

It was felt that this sequence was not only more natural to children but also that it gave them help from the context; and in emphasising primarily 'meaning' and fluency it discouraged the unprofitable habit of 'word-calling'. In practice, however, the sentence method frequently—perhaps nearly always—became a whole word method, partly because the component parts of a sentence are essential to the whole. It was often observed that less able children, in particular, really needed to reduce the sentence to a more manageable unit. And if, as now seems likely, children generally break down even the word in order to find clues which help them, then a large unit of recognition like a sentence would, in this context, be inappropriate.

However, we cannot really abolish the whole word as a tentative unit of recognition in the very early stages of learn-

[9] Geoffrey R. Roberts, *Reading in Primary Schools* (London, Routledge & Kegan Paul, 1969), p. 11.

ing to read. We cannot escape the fact that our written language includes not only words in which single letters and clusters of letters have a regular sound correspondence, but also words in which such correspondence is totally irregular. Leaving aside for the moment i.t.a. and other approaches which are based on the principle of eliminating this irregularity, we also find that an exclusively phonic approach is ineffective in the early stage of learning to read. In the circumstances, we must surely reach the conclusion that neither the one nor the other provides, *by itself*, the whole answer.

The practical consequences of this dichotomy are not, however, as open-ended as they seem. In the first place, it should be made clear that the use of the component parts of a word to assist in its identification does not represent a return to the old phonic method of 'the pig in a wig did a jig' variety. Daniels and Diack, for example, do not imply that their analytic phonic word approach is based on this principle.

The point at issue is that instead of eschewing, in word recognition, the help of the sound or appearance of certain letters or letter combinations, the teacher encourages the child to use them (when possible) as a positive means of identification. For example, when using the *Janet and John* scheme in a reception class some years ago, the teacher told the children a delightful story about a rude little man with his toes turned up and his tongue stuck out, who looked like this—'t'. Few children thereafter had any difficulty in distinguishing 'Janet' from 'John', because 'Janet' ended with a picture of the rude little man. The fact that 'toes' and 'tongue' also begin with the sound of the letter gave the teacher an admirable opportunity for introducing some early phonic training quite naturally and informally—and very valuably.

At the beginning therefore words, and perhaps little phrases which have personal significance, such as 'my dog', will be presented in look-and-say form. It would be hard to find a leading authority on the initial teaching of reading who could not approve of this. But right from the start the importance of clues in the recognition of a word should be stressed. The clue may be a picture, the shape of the word, its length if this is a distinguishing feature, the presence of a double letter, the long tail at the beginning, the little man with his toes turned up. When letter/sound correspondence can be introduced informally and conversationally—without pressing it in any sense as a drill—there is no reason why the teacher should not make use of the opportunity.

This approach does not deny the contribution of look-and-say as *one element*, probably a very important one, in the presentation of early reading material. It does, however, add another element and in this we may agree with Donald Moyle: 'While one would certainly not underestimate the difficulties involved in letter recognition, the evidence available seems to point to the conclusion that it cannot but be helpful to make the child aware, in some way, that words are composed of letters from the very beginning of instruction.'[10] The children's attention should therefore be drawn to the *appearance* of certain letter forms, with or without their associated sounds according to whether this is appropriate.

Roberts goes even further:

... look-and-say should be regarded as part of the preparatory approach which should be clearly differentiated from word identification and learning to read in the true sense of the phrases. Indeed, where look-and-say persists beyond the necessary preparatory period the children will learn to read by other means, in that they will learn to make correspondences between letters and sounds for themselves. Later, when they have learned the fundamental skills of reading, then look-and-say techniques can be used to achieve a quicker, easier rate of reading.[11]

Almost any look-and-say reading scheme can be adapted to make use of clues, including letters, in word recognition; though it must be admitted that some schemes which are very resolutely based on the sentence method make this more difficult. However, if we accept that clues in words do help children, we must reduce the sentence to a unit which is small enough for the child to accommodate.

[10] Moyle, *The Teaching of Reading*, p. 42.
[11] Roberts, op. cit., p. 5.

VISUAL AND AUDITORY DISCRIMINATION

If children are to learn, or be trained, to see the differences in
the written patterns of words and to recognise the correspondence between these patterns and the sounds that they hear,
it is plain that in order to help them we must know something
about their powers of visual and auditory discrimination. It
is now thought that these abilities are partly innate and partly
acquired. At one time it was thought that they depended
almost entirely upon maturation and could not be appreciably
hastened by training of any kind. More recent evidence, however, strongly suggests that this is not the case and that training,
provided it is directed towards that part of the child's acquisition of these skills which may respond to it, may indeed play
a significant part.

With regard to visual discrimination it used to be widely
believed that before the age of about six children's eyes were
not sufficiently developed physically and physiologically to
enable them to make the fine visual distinctions that reading
requires. It now seems fairly firmly established that this is
not so. In studies which have been undertaken to investigate
this question, children starting school have generally been
found to be capable of seeing quite fine distinctions, though
they may not immediately register some of the very small
differences in letter shapes.

They have not, however, been found capable of remembering the *sequence* of letter shapes in a word and they do have
difficulty in distinguishing between inverted letters such as
'b' and 'd'. In these skills, maturation may well be significant;
but it is also possible that helping the child to look for
similarities and differences in words, and for 'clues' (which is
not the same thing as expecting him to memorise, at an early
stage, all the letter shapes and their associated sounds), assist-
ing him to form the habit of left/right sequence, giving him
the opportunity of seeing and forming letters, and informally
familiarising him, where this is appropriate, with the association between certain sounds and letters or groups of letters—
that training of this kind will help to precipitate the learning
which his degree of maturation makes possible. In a careful
study of reading readiness Downing and Thackray say that the

weight of evidence 'seems to favour the view that the perceptual activities of children should not be under-estimated, and more consideration must be given to the extent to which we can develop these various abilities through training'.[12]

Concerning auditory discrimination, it is evident that this may not be fully developed before a mental age of about seven to seven and a half years. It has been found that the sounds which are heard in the middle and lower frequencies can be distinguished earlier than those in the high frequencies. It is not, therefore, a situation in which the discrimination of *all* sounds is more or less uniformly uncertain for the young child: *some* sounds can be distinguished at an earlier age and others cannot. Goodacre refers to some evidence which teachers may find very helpful here:

> Work by Poole (1934) is often quoted which shows the *latest age* at which consonant sounds appear in normal children's speech.
>
> 'Age $3\frac{1}{2}$ sounds mastered b - p - m - w - h
> Age $4\frac{1}{2}$ sounds mastered d - t - n - g - k - ng - y
> Age $5\frac{1}{2}$ sounds mastered f
> Age $6\frac{1}{2}$ sounds mastered v - th (as in then) - sh - zh - 1
> Age $7\frac{1}{2}$ sounds mastered s - z - r - th (thin) - wh - ch - (j)'
>
> What is important to note is that the sound acquisition in children's speech is progressive and that amongst normal children the particular speech sounds may not be correctly used until as late as seven or eight.[13]

Dr Goodacre goes on to reinforce this with recent evidence.

The conclusions reached from all the work done on auditory discrimination therefore support the view

(i) that at five the normal child can distinguish between the sound patterns of whole words;
(ii) that the discrimination of the sounds of individual letters takes place progressively, until it is generally complete by a mental age of about seven to seven and a half;

[12] John Downing and D. V. Thackray, *Reading Readiness* (London, University of London Press, 1971), p. 61.
[13] Goodacre, op. cit., p. 75.

(iii) that the ability to break down the whole word into the sounds of all its constituent letters, and to arrange them into correct sequence, is very much a maturational process. The ability to do this will clearly develop first with short, phonically regular words, and many children in the First School, given appropriate training, can analyse the sounds of words like 'but' and 'in' and arrange them in their correct order both in reading and in writing. But more complex arrangements of sounds will naturally be longer delayed and the teacher must judge this capacity very much in accordance with the ability and maturational level of individual children.

These conclusions have important implications for phonic teaching, and they suggest certain lines of approach:

(i) From the beginning of reading instruction, the teacher may informally draw the child's attention to the sounds of some of the letters and letter combinations, beginning with those that are thought to be within the child's auditory capacity at this stage.

(ii) As the child's auditory discrimination develops, this practice may be extended and undertaken by the teacher more systematically.

(iii) Help in establishing good left/right orientation is important.

(iv) Familiarity with the sounds of letters and letter combinations will be of great assistance to the child when he reaches the maturational level of being able to analyse the constituent sounds of words and assemble them in the correct sequence.

These considerations will be reflected in the practical teaching suggestions that are included in some detail in later chapters.

Chapter 3

Learning to Read – other Important Factors

It is well established that in addition to the skills and abilities associated with seeing and hearing, there are a number of other factors which play a vital part in a child's capacity to learn to read. Among the most significant of these are memory, intelligence, language and environment, and emotional and physical factors.

MEMORY

Whatever means is used in word recognition—whether it concerns the shape or appearance of the whole word, or a distinctive feature of some constituent part—the child must ultimately store the image in his memory so that it can be instantly recalled. Moreover, he must store not only the visual image but also its associated sound. Lovell explains that memory depends to a great extent upon general intelligence, since in order to remember something one must be able to learn it in the first place.[1] Some children will therefore remember more readily and more clearly than others, but apart from recognising this obvious truth we need to concern ourselves with the strategies children appear to employ to help them in remembering words.

Here again we find ourselves returning, partly at any rate, to the question of 'clues'. Many of these have already been mentioned—length of word, picture association, the peculiarity of certain letters, etc.—and in addition there is frequent reference to evidence which strongly suggests that the first and last

[1] Lovell, *Educational Psychology and Children*, p. 119.

letters of a word play a major part in helping a child to identify and ultimately remember it. Goodacre attaches particular importance to this: '. . . recent research . . . suggests that children pay less attention to the overall shape of words than to the beginning and last *letters*. The white space before and after words helps not only to define the form of words but also to bring out the clarity of beginning and end letters in words.'[2]

This indicates that children should have the opportunity of becoming familiar with letter shapes from a very early stage. This is not a matter of phonic 'drill' or indeed even of 'formal' phonics, to begin with. But if children can physically handle wooden or cardboard letter shapes and play with them and talk about them and perhaps draw round them, these shapes will acquire familiarity. This could greatly help children to remember them and thus to use them as clues when they see them in a word. It is not suggested, however, that at this stage they should be required to learn the letter names. A letter could be named conversationally if in discussion this happened to arise, but it would be unreasonable to expect children to memorise all the letter names to begin with; and even if they could it is doubtful if it would help word recognition. It is the *shape* of the letter that is likely to be helpful as a clue, not, at first, its phonic interpretation.

It seems certain that a child is less likely to remember a word if it is not part of the vocabulary he normally uses. This hypothesis will be developed a little more when the importance of language is considered, but in the context of memory the point underlines the importance of discussion and of the extension of experience from which profitable discussion may spring. It underlines also the need to examine the vocabulary of the reading scheme, if one is used. There has been some criticism recently of the rather cosy suburban nature of the material found in many of the commonly used reading schemes, though sometimes it is less the vocabulary that is at fault than the representation of the characters and their doings which are remote from the everyday lives of so many children. Indeed, it is not only in helping children to remember words that the reality and relevance of reading material are important. Without the incentive of situations and experiences with which the

[2] Goodacre, *Children and Learning to Read*, p. 60.

child can identify himself and which therefore can have interest and meaning for him it is difficult to see how he will be motivated to make the effort that learning to read undoubtedly requires.

INTELLIGENCE

The relationship between intelligence and the ability to learn to read is so complex and involves such an extensive range of qualifying factors that any depth of understanding of this whole question requires the most detailed and specialised study. No more can be attempted here than to summarise the general conclusions that seem valid in directly practical terms, to serve as an immediate guide and a 'prompt' for the teacher when she is planning and executing her reading programme.

It would hardly be denied that a child with a generous endowment of intelligence will normally find it much easier to learn to read than the child whose mental capacity is very limited. However, this leads us to two very vital qualifications which are so apparent that only their importance justifies their mention.

(i) The intelligent child may experience difficulty in learning to read because of other handicaps such as environmental or emotional disadvantage, language disability, and so on.

(ii) The child of even very limited intelligence can, in favourable circumstances, learn to read surprisingly well.

The inescapable fact is that the better the teacher knows her children and the more she is able in practice to compensate for specific disadvantages (i.e. linguistic deprivation) the more likely she is to achieve some degree of success. Clearly it would be illusory to suggest (*a*) that any teacher can know every child so intimately that she can diagnose exactly his requirements and make available to him a kind of teaching package containing all the necessary ingredients in the right proportions; or (*b*) that even if some, or most, of these requirements are reasonably well known it is within the teacher's power to compensate in school for all a child's disadvantages so that his natural endowment of intelligence can be used to full capacity.

However, despite all these qualifications there seems little doubt that intelligence really is significant. Linguistic or other disadvantages aside, the less able child *will* have more difficulty in learning to read than the child who has good general intelligence to help him. It is nevertheless interesting to note that there seems to be a closer correlation between measured I.Q. and reading attainment in earlier years than there is later; but as reading ability progresses general intelligence appears to contribute less to word recognition and more to comprehension. This suggests that at the beginning, when 'reading' is inevitably very dependent upon word recognition, the child's intelligence is more strongly directed towards his mastery of this early skill than it will be later on when other abilities besides word recognition become more important.

When word recognition has been perfected with sufficient skill for it to be established as a 'habit', the child of lower mental ability may 'read' almost as fluently as the child with a much higher measured I.Q. But by then comprehension and meaning contribute much more to reading attainment and the relation between intelligence and comprehension assumes greater significance. The position is summarised thus by Moyle: '. . . although there would seem to be a relationship between general ability and reading attainment, it is by no means a perfect one. There are other variables present such as visual skills and linguistic development and these more specific abilities apparently increase in importance as reading attainment grows over the years.'[3]

In practical terms this suggests that an effective preparatory period may greatly benefit the child who is slow to begin, whether this is due to limited general intelligence or to other influences which may be inhibiting a more able child from making a start. The intelligent child without any particular difficulties is usually easy to identify and he will move forward at a more rapid pace. For the others, the preparatory period will vary in length, and in getting to know her children as well as possible the teacher has more chance of arriving at an assessment of particular problems or circumstances. One of the more helpful indications which may emerge with time is that the child of good general intelligence may well show this

[3] Moyle, *The Teaching of Reading*, p. 47.

in activities other than reading. The teacher may then be able to direct her attention rather more towards trying to uncover some of the other possible causes of a slow start in reading.

At a later stage, when comprehension and meaning play a greater part, the teacher would recognise that this presents the child of limited ability with more difficulty. Careful selection of reading material could help here and encouragement to the child to apply his more limited reading skill to material in which he has a direct opportunity to follow some particular interest. For example, a child who is especially interested in cars may be more strongly motivated to develop his skill with simple books about cars and with card apparatus specially made to fit his particular preoccupation. He may well be helped to make the extra effort with this kind of reading material than with the next book in the reading scheme.

Opinion is still very divided on the question of whether or not a child's 'natural endowment' of intelligence can be developed or even increased by training. But observation and common sense must surely encourage the belief that if a child of apparently limited intelligence can be sufficiently well supported in a stimulating and sympathetic learning environment, where his personal interests and concerns are taken much into account, he may be helped to apply whatever natural endowment he has in such a way that he can find satisfaction in personal achievement; and this is especially true of reading, because so much else depends upon it. Of course the attainment of this goal is an ideal and we do not pretend that we have magic wands which ensure that we always reach it. But this has never prevented the good teacher from trying and sometimes from achieving a degree of success.

At the other end of the scale, the child whose reading skill is well advanced and who in all probability has the advantage of natural ability should now have the kind of reading material which will stretch him and cause him to develop comprehension and real fluency. Children sometimes think that the end of the reading scheme marks the end of having to 'learn to read'. In an initial sense this, of course, is true; but in a genuinely educational sense it is only a beginning. The teacher who can inspire the able child to see it in this way will be doing him a lasting service.

LANGUAGE AND ENVIRONMENT

It is now almost a truism to say that a child cannot be expected to read words which are not already part of his spoken vocabulary. Many children when they start school have already acquired a surprisingly large spoken vocabulary—generally estimated at between 2,000 and 3,000 words. However, there are immense variations between individual children, and there are also great differences between the number of words which children know and in theory *could* use, and the number which in fact they *do* use in their everyday speech.

Perhaps it may be valid in this context to suggest a distinction between a child's vocabulary and his language. The former implies a kind of computational exercise of counting words; the latter suggests the child's everyday use of words, the *language* with which he is at ease and which he uses with comfortable familiarity for all his daily practical, intellectual and communicative purposes.

It is surely his language that really matters when it comes to learning to read. The child whose linguistic skill is fairly sophisticated, who can almost unconsciously call upon a variety of words and phrases with which to express himself, who has something to say because his range of experience has made it possible for him to see and do all kinds of things and then discuss them with articulate adults and peers, who has handled books and has seen and heard the words in them even if he cannot actually read them himself, has an enormous built-in advantage because language, as a vehicle of self expression, is already part of his everyday life. Now that he is at school he really takes it for granted that he is going to learn to read— if, indeed, he is not already well on the way to doing so. To him it is a natural and expected step that he should now learn how to interpret the written form of the language with which he is so familiar.

Yet the child who has not had these advantages is in a very different situation. Hitherto his everyday language has served him well for the demands which have been made upon him within a fairly restricted field of activity and communication. But when he starts school he finds himself having to meet new and very unfamiliar verbal requirements. He may be asked, sometimes daily, to tell his teacher and other children what he has been doing. It may be difficult enough for him to think of something that will stand comparison with the visit to the zoo which Paul has just recounted; but added to this the child must try to find the words, on the spur of the moment, to make a coherent public statement, a form of communication quite different from that which until now he has met in his daily spontaneous conversation.

He is introduced, almost at once, to the written word in some form, perhaps the weather chart or a piece of word and picture matching apparatus. He has, of course, seen many written words before, labels in shops, advertisements on buses, captions on the television. But he has probably never been asked to *do* anything with these words; they have been quite impersonal. Now he is required, perhaps for the first time, to be personally concerned with them—he is going to have to learn what they are, and they may not even be pronounced in a way which he recognises.

He sees books. He may like them; they are attractive—but they are new to him. His teacher reads a story, and this may never have happened before either. The Plowden Committee reported that in 29 per cent of homes there were only five books or less.[4] The very notion is new of connecting language, as this child understands it, with books, let alone of associating himself with the possibility of reading them. Why, in any case, should he immediately see the value of doing so? The people he has known until now do not often appear to feel the need to read books. Why should it occur to him that he should? The gulf between reading and his language and experience is immense.

A picture of extremes has been painted in order to try to analyse the nature of the problem facing the linguistically deprived child when he first encounters a situation in which words, spoken as well as written, assume an entirely new dimension. We can see the nature of the gap which has to be bridged before we can expect 'reading' to have relevance or interest to the child whose language and experience have not yet fitted him for the task. It is not difficult, in this context, to

4 Plowden Report, *Children and Their Primary Schools* (London, H.M.S.O., 1967), para. 97.

recognise the importance in school of the kind of activities and new experiences which we try to give the children in order that they may have more things to talk about, opportunities for hearing and using a more extended language and the stimulation of doing interesting things which we hope will help to make learning more of a pleasure than a chore. It must be repeated, however, that the provision of this kind of environment is not, by itself, enough. Vital though it is, it will not enable the child to 'discover' how to read. We must still, within this environment, teach him how to do so.

Apart from linguistic and experiential deprivation, the most important environmental influence which affects a child's ability to learn to read is believed to be the support and sympathy he is given at home. Lack of this is frequently associated with unfavourable socio-economic conditions because the anxiety of personal and financial burdens, the limited education of parents, an overworked mother and the family's inevitable preoccupation with pressing daily problems are clearly likely to have adverse effects on a child's commitment to any learning situation. However, there can also be lack of interest in very favourable material conditions where parents are so busy being 'successful' that they have barely time to spare for the child's affairs; and undoubtedly there can be over-anxiety for the child's progress among parents at the higher socio-economic levels which leads them to overburden the child with too much pressure for him to succeed.

It would be unrealistic to claim that the teacher can compensate entirely for a lack of sympathetic support at home, whatever the cause may be. Her awareness of its effect, however, can help her to understand something of the child's difficulties and the very fact of her understanding them can be of great value. In adjusting her approach and her requirements when dealing with the child whom she knows to be under domestic pressure she can avoid adding to his difficulties even if she cannot eliminate them. It cannot but help for her to appreciate all the influences which may have an effect on his ability to learn to read; and she may take comfort from the conclusion reached in research undertaken for the N.F.E.R. by a team investigating reading attainment in infant schools representing both deprived and socially favoured areas of London:

'. . . while the home influence is predominant, the school influence is by no means negligible.'[5]

EMOTIONAL FACTORS

In Schonell's view 'ability in reading as with other school skills is just as sensitive to positive and negative emotional attitudes. The vital need is to make clear to all concerned the significance of emotional and personality factors in promoting or inhibiting progress in reading.'[6]

What then are these emotional and personality factors which exercise such a strong influence?

Schonell's reference to 'attitudes' draws attention to the root of the matter. So much exhortation has been given to teachers in recent years about the importance of creating the kind of atmosphere in which children will want to learn that there is no need here to restate the case. Motivation, we accept, is crucial. Attitudes, however, are subject to other influences besides a stimulating school atmosphere. A child may very much enjoy school and find in it plenty of interesting things to do; and yet if through lack of application or for any other reason he does not want to make the effort to learn to read (or cannot make it) he may consciously or subconsciously avoid it.

The teacher's strategy here must be twofold. She must first of all try to help him to recognise that once he can read new horizons are open to him; and nothing is as easy to say as this, while almost nothing is more difficult to achieve in practice. It is a case where advice is easy, but putting it into effect is something quite different.

Of course the teacher must try in every possible way to interest the child in the printed word with books and attractively presented reading materials and all the other familiar items that come out of her professional bag. Sometimes she will be

---

[5] Brian Cane and Jane Smithers, ed. Gabriel Chanan, *The Roots of Reading* (Slough, National Foundation for Educational Research, 1971), p. 81.

[6] Schonell, *The Psychology and Teaching of Reading*, p. 41.

successful, and sometimes she will not; and then she goes on trying. The only advice that is of any value is that she must have patience, persistence, imagination, and understanding as far as she possibly can of everything affecting the child that might help to explain his problem. Even a limited degree of success will in the end encourage both the teacher and the child.

The second of the teacher's strategies presents no such dilemma. She must have the kind of organisation which makes it quite impossible for the child's avoidance of particular reading activities to go unnoticed. If organisation is at all shaky it is only too easy for this to happen, especially if the class is large and the programme extremely fluid. But it must not happen, and it cannot happen with a properly planned and organised reading programme.

Children's attitudes can also be influenced by other aspects of temperament and personality. The child who lacks confidence or who is extremely sensitive will often be unwilling to try to read because he is afraid that what he says might be wrong. Patience and sympathetic handling on the part of the teacher will overcome this; but it can take time. Sometimes the child who appears to be over-confident and who guesses wildly because he feels he has to show that he can do it, is in fact unconsciously using this as a cover for his fear of being unsuccessful. Then there is the child who is a butterfly, who flits from activity to activity without alighting upon any of them for long enough to absorb anything; and the other child who applies himself with a determination so grim that failure to achieve early success assumes the proportions of a major disaster. The calm, balanced, happy child, though not altogether rare, is the most favoured of mortals. Whatever other difficulties he may face in learning to read, problems of temperament will not be among them.

Certainly temperament and emotional difficulties have a recognisable influence on a child's progress in reading. But success breeds success, and time and adequate preparation are great allies. Above all, perhaps, the teacher's observation, her common sense and her ability to establish a sound and sympathetic pupil/teacher relationship will, with most children, be of immense value in counteracting emotional ill effects. In extreme cases, however, it may be necessary to refer a child for specialist help.

PHYSICAL FACTORS

Obvious physical factors which will retard a child's progress in reading are defects of eyesight, hearing and speech. All of these need specialist help which fortunately is readily available. The teacher, however, has to be something of a diagnostician, particularly with regard to defective sight or hearing. Unless these are severe they may escape early detection, more especially with the able child whose progress may obscure defects which are in fact limiting his real capacity. Careful observation on the part of the teacher may help to bring these to light and if she is at all suspicious she should certainly err on the side of safety in referring the child for expert examination.

Fatigue and ill-health can also retard a child and if ill-health results in prolonged or frequent absence from school his progress in reading will suffer. Even children whose length of schooling is curtailed because they are the youngest in an age group are known to be at a disadvantage in reading attainment. Evidence for this emerged in the National Child Development Study undertaken in 1958.[7] For children whose schooling is much interrupted, the problem is exacerbated; and it may be quite as acute for the child with poor health, not always ill enough to be kept at home, but tired and unable to make much effort when he is in school. The teacher must try, as far as she can, to give these children such extra help and encouragement as the many other demands on her time will realistically allow.

There is some evidence to suggest that children whose dominant hand and eye do not coincide are at a disadvantage in learning to read. Moyle explains the position very clearly:

The majority of people have established a preference for the right hand and the right eye has become the dominant or leading eye. A further smaller percentage have established the co-ordination of the left hand and left eye. Some people,

[7] Ronald Davie, 'Reading at the Infant Stage: Some Results from the National Child Development Study (1958 Cohort),' in J. C. Daniels (ed.), *Reading: Problems and Perspectives* (United Kingdom Reading Association, 1970), p. 31.

however, have preferred hands and dominant eyes on opposite sides which makes difficulties with regard to the co-ordination necessary in reading the printed word or in writing. This condition does not necessarily lead to reading failure but would seem to be found in a far higher percentage of poor readers than in the population at large.[8]

The writer recollects a particularly noticeable case of a 6-year-old boy who was left-handed, and who was blind in his left eye. He experienced extreme difficulty in learning to read, and indeed was still a non-reader when he moved on to the junior school. He also had very little hand/eye co-ordination and his ability to write was accordingly severely restricted. No general conclusions can be drawn from an isolated example; the child in any case came from a linguistically deprived background and was physically and socially undeveloped in comparison with his peers. But the point at issue is that the condition of opposing dominance of hand and eye does exist, and though the teacher cannot alter it she may in some cases be able to take it into account in her expectations and in her judgement of a child's progress.

It would not be out of place to add a word or two on sex difference, if only to draw attention to the very conflicting evidence that is available on this point. The results from the National Child Development Study already quoted plainly uphold the view that girls have the advantage. 'Whatever the reasons, it is clear that the fact of the girls' superiority in this area should be borne in mind if verbal reasoning tests or similar measures are used as a basis for assessing [reading] ability on entry to junior schools.'[9] Moyle on the other hand quotes three Ministry of Education surveys of 1948, 1952 and 1956, which 'seem to show that reading attainment among boys is slightly superior to that among girls', but 'most surveys prior to this time and also the 1954 section of the Kent Survey had shown a slight advantage to the girls'. He adds that 'this conflicting evidence can only lead us to assume that the Watts-Vernon test employed by the Ministry gives boys a greater opportunity to do well in it than it does the girls. Vice versa

[8] Moyle, *The Teaching of Reading*, p. 61.
[9] Davie, op. cit., p. 30.

it may also be that some other reading tests favour the girls.'
Moyle wisely concludes that 'the evidence available clearly
demonstrates that sex difference is not a significant factor in
its effect upon the process of learning to read'.[10] In this area,
at least, it seems that the teacher may still pay her penny and
take her choice.

[10] Moyle, op. cit., p. 62–3.

Chapter 4

Reading Readiness

The controversy which for some time has been associated with the term 'reading readiness' has come about partly because of the way in which the developmental theory of learning used to be interpreted and partly because of the failure of some of the protagonists to define precisely what they mean by reading readiness when arguing the case.

When Piaget's developmental theory first became popular it gave rise to the widely accepted view that there were certain clearly defined stages of intellectual development and that until a child, largely by a process of maturation, reached a stage appropriate to a particular form of learning he could not undertake that learning whatever the teacher did. Although the results of Piaget's early investigations into the stages of children's intellectual development certainly seemed to support this view we must remember that he was not at that time specifically associating his investigations with teaching methods. At all events, one of the consequences of the acceptance of the developmental theory was a wholehearted belief that reading readiness was the result, in effect, of maturation alone.

Until a child reached this stage it was useless to try to teach him to read because he *simply could not do so*. Furthermore, it was feared that if a teacher failed to recognise this and tried to make the child learn to read before he was ready for it his future emotional reaction to reading might be more or less permanently disturbed.

At the same time the emphasis on the importance of a child-centred education and on the development of 'the whole child' gave support to the practice of encouraging the child 'to develop as an individual' in a stimulating learning environment without worrying him by concerning him with the printed word for which he was not yet ready. In due course he would reach the stage of 'reading readiness' and this would be fairly recognisable because the child would show evidence of wanting to read. He would be interested in books, he would ask about the captions, he would want to know about printed words— and at this point he would be ready to begin. It was thought that this would generally happen when a mental age of about six to six and a half years was reached.

Since then, however, the developmental theory has been less rigidly interpreted, and particularly with regard to reading. A great deal of work has been done in this field and the earlier belief in the existence of an almost wholly maturational stage of 'reading readiness' is no longer acceptable. The opening paragraph of *Reading Readiness* by Downing and Thackray clearly defines the modern view.

> The term 'readiness' for any kind of learning refers to the stage firstly, when the child can learn easily and without emotional strain, and secondly, when the child can learn profitably because efforts at teaching give gratifying results. Note that 'readiness' does not necessarily imply that a child achieves this state only through growth or maturation. He may also arrive at readiness through having completed the prior learning on which the new learning will be based.[1]

Mackay, in describing part of a preparatory programme, puts it like this: 'The teacher . . . is not waiting for readiness to happen, she is drawing children nearer and nearer to the point at which they wish to participate.'[2] And Roberts is refreshingly forthright. 'It is not just a matter of [teachers] letting children wallow in a rich environment; they must use that environment to bring children closer and closer to the interpretation of print.'[3]

From statements such as these it can be seen that there is now a great deal more emphasis on the value of training in helping the child to reach the point when he can begin to read. The developmental theory is not denied nor is the immensely

[1] Downing and Thackray, *Reading Readiness*, p. 9.

[2] David Mackay, 'Breakthrough to Literacy', in John Merritt (ed.), *Reading and the Curriculum* (London, Ward Lock Educational for U.K.R.A., 1971), p. 228.

[3] Roberts, *Reading in Primary Schools*, p. 23.

valuable work of Piaget discredited. Growth and maturation are still accepted as vitally important in learning and indeed the fact that *stages* of development exist is not seriously questioned. What *is* questioned, to the extent of being no longer generally acceptable, is that nothing whatever can be done to precipitate the child's movement from one stage to the next. Maturation plays its part; it is clear that the 6-year-old cannot read as the 10-year-old with comparable gifts and advantages can read. But growth and maturation are not thought to be, by themselves, the only limiting factors in learning. Children will not learn to read simply by maturing. They must be taught as well. Thus it is not suggested that there is no such thing as a stage of reading readiness. The point at which a child really does begin to read is the point at which the factors that have hitherto prevented him from doing so have been sufficiently modified, and the skills and abilities he needs for the task have been sufficiently developed *and* trained, to make reading possible. This represents the stage of reading readiness.

Some of the influences which until now have made him unready to read and some of the skills and abilities which were not sufficiently advanced before, have been susceptible to the teacher's actions and her handling of the child. She has taken steps to compensate for linguistic deprivation. She has made available materials which, with her help, have encouraged left/right orientation and have given the child clues for word recognition. The materials have been presented in such a way that the child's fixation span has not been limited by inappropriate print or word arrangement. She has given confidence to the timid and has widened the horizons of those whose experience was severely restricted.

She has not, of course, been successful to the same degree with every child and some, for various reasons, still have a long way to go. But the vitally important consideration is that the teacher has not just provided 'a stimulating learning environment' and then waited for the stage of reading readiness to appear. She has done a very great deal to cause it to appear and she will continue to provide a suitable preparatory programme for those children who still need such a programme in that form.

Moyle reports an interesting investigation which supports the value of training.

Scottish children seem to be as much as eighteen months in advance of their American peers at the tender age of six and a half years in the sphere of reading according to Taylor (1950).[4] The only substantial difference between the two groups of children studied was the fact that the Scottish children had entered school earlier and thus it can only be concluded that reading readiness can be affected by training and is not solely dependent upon maturation.[5]

In addition to the school of thought which admits the value of training in helping to precipitate reading readiness, there is another which holds the extreme view that there is no such thing as reading readiness at all and the whole idea should be abandoned. Its exponents seem to recommend that preparatory reading programmes should be abolished and that children should be taught to read in a more direct manner from the time they start school. Downing and Thackray report on an American study in 1965 from which emerged much doubt on the validity of this approach. The results in fact pointed to:

the real value of the concept of reading readiness. Mass teaching of all children at age five or even at age six ignores important individual differences in children's abilities and styles of learning. . . . Complete abolition of the concept of reading readiness could be a retrograde step if it led to pressuring unwilling children into reading. Therefore our conclusion is that the reading readiness concept should be retained, but modified to take account of modern developments in this field.[6]

There is one aspect of teaching children to read which had little mention in the past but which modern research has thrown into greater relief. It concerns the need for the teacher to take positive measures to help children to understand certain elements of the reading process which are so basic that as adults we have all long since forgotten ever having en-

---

[4] No known connection with the writer!
[5] Moyle, *The Teaching of Reading*, p. 68.
[6] Downing and Thackray, op. cit., p. 70.

countered them. We are inclined to take it for granted, for example, that all 5-year-olds realise what reading is. But it seems that all of them do not. Some of these children do not appreciate that when an adult is reading a book he is translating certain symbols and patterns either silently to himself or aloud to his hearers. We assume that if a child looks at a book which has pictures and captions, he knows which part of the total presentation represents the printed word and which does not. Certainly it is true that some children at five appreciate these things; but if their experience until then has not put this kind of understanding in their way, our assumptions about their ideas of reading may be quite inaccurate.

Thus it seems that many young children really do not know what 'reading' means. They have not had occasion ever to consider that we may look at one kind of visual pattern (i.e. a picture) and having absorbed it by sight our action is complete except that we may think or talk about it; and that we look at another kind of visual pattern (a picture and writing), part of which we then translate into words—not just any suitable descriptive words, but *particular* words which we have 'read'. The point is so clearly described by Mackay that it is well worth quoting at length.

Many children arrive at school with very little idea of what written language is; some children may not understand the difference between the text and the illustrations in a picture story book, nor the connection between the marks on the page and the words spoken aloud by the teacher when she reads stories. Even though our children are surrounded by written language in shops, on the television screen, in the streets, in magazines, newspapers and books, it remains for most of them a mysterious code and they have no clue as to how to decipher it.

At first you should read to the children from picture story books and discuss with them precisely what you are doing, helping them to understand the difference between *reading* a story and *telling* a story. Children should be encouraged to discuss the differences between the text and the picture. They sometimes think that the line of print under illustrations is no more than a decorative border.

Next, the connection between the printed marks and spoken language should be established by saying something like 'These marks show me what I must say.' If you say 'This word says . . .' or 'This letter says . . .' make sure that children understand that you are speaking figuratively (since the written marks cannot and do not *say* anything).

Another aspect of the writing system that should be dealt with at this time is the directionality of written English. When you are reading show children that you start at the top left-hand corner and read each time from left to right, from the top line to the bottom, following the lines of print with your finger to show the direction. Large wall charts of nursery rhymes are particularly easy to follow and establish this point well. . . .

All writings put up round the room . . . help to reinforce knowledge about written language but they need to be brought to children's attention frequently.[7]

A further point is that we use words connected with reading in the belief that all children know what these words mean —for example 'sentence', 'word', 'letter', 'sound'. For many children, we must in fact explain the meaning of such words most carefully and in a number of different contexts so that the child can extract their precise meaning. Sometimes an alternative word may be better to begin with, if there is an alternative which conveys the meaning more easily. For example, even quite able children find 'sound' difficult to understand in connection with dissecting the spoken word into its phonic or phonemic components. If the teacher says 'What is the first sound in "sat"?', this may well mean nothing to them. But if she says 'What is the first *noise* you make when you say "sat". . . . What is the next noise. . . ?', children have been found to be much more likely to make the connection.

Clearly it is important that we should pay great attention to the question of helping children to understand what reading is, what we mean when we use certain words, the purpose of learning to read and what they may expect of the whole enterprise. An interesting comment is quoted in this connection

[7] David Mackay, Brian Thompson and Pamela Schaub, *Breakthrough to Literacy: Teacher's Manual* (London, Longman for the Schools Council, 1970), pp. 6–7.

by Goodacre. 'Mason (1967) in the United States studied the attitudes of 178 pre-schoolers learning to read and found that most of them thought they could already "read". He concluded that "one of the first steps in learning to read is learning that one doesn't already know how. This seems to be a step in learning to read or in reading readiness which has been neglected. . . ." " [8]

There is no doubt that it would be most helpful if the teacher could be given a clear formula which she could apply in determining for each child when the stage of reading readiness is reached. Unfortunately this is not possible, partly because our present state of knowledge of reading readiness is not precise enough, and partly because so much depends upon the individual child. The most that one can do is to suggest some broad guide-lines, accepting that ultimately the teacher must depend largely upon her own observation and judgement.

One guide-line is a child's reaction to the reading material on wall charts and other classroom displays and the extent to which he participates in interpreting them. This applies also to individual apparatus and the other preparatory reading activities in which the children engage. From some of these, it will be apparent whether the child has developed the capacity to distinguish between the visual patterns of words, and whether his auditory discrimination is adequate.

Another guide, which with some children is very clear and with others less so, is the degree of interest and motivation they exhibit—their concern with books, their enquiries about the printed words, their evident wish to be able to read them by themselves. Additionally, the child's linguistic skill, the facility with which he is able to use words, is known to be important. But it can involve a very delicate judgement, since a reserved child may appear to be inarticulate and an articulate child whose experience has favoured his linguistic development may for other reasons be far from ready to leave the preparatory period behind him. As Moyle remarks, '. . . the child should have a good vocabulary and a wide range of experience but we might well ask—how many words and experiences, which words and which experiences?' [9]

[8] Goodacre, *Children and Learning to Read*, p. 4.
[9] Moyle, op. cit., p. 71.

However, linguistic skill must be given due weight and the teacher's knowledge of the child as a person may well help her here. Other indications are whether the child has the confidence to try, whether he can concentrate, and whether he can with reasonable certainty recognise some of the words which he encounters frequently.

Thus there can be no clear-cut answer to the question of when a child is ready to begin reading. Moreover, it depends very much upon what is meant by being 'ready to begin reading'. If this is taken to mean that there will come a day on which a decision can be made to put away the 'pre-reading activities' and take out a reading book, to change over to a 'systematic' programme of reading instruction, then the point of reading readiness will probably be impossible to determine. The stage of reading readiness is more likely to manifest itself as a time when one set of skills and abilities and attitudes is merged into another and the child then responds to an approach which is the natural outcome, and in many ways a continuation, of the activities and the experiences of the preparatory period. It is the time when the child seems to recognise that reading is no longer a mystery. It is, to him, an accomplishment which is definable and which can be admitted to the category of 'things I am learning to do'.

In accepting the value of a preparatory period during which the child approaches the stage of reading readiness, we must accept also that teaching in this preparatory period is crucial. The Scottish Council on Education has made the point quite explicitly:

It is important to realise that reading readiness does not come by nature. The child brought up in a savage tribe that has no written records can have no reading readiness . . . reading readiness is not the product of maturation alone. Some degree of mental development and of other abilities and qualities must be attained before the reading task can be successfully performed, but the teacher's work cannot be accomplished by waiting on Nature.[10]

[10] Quoted by E. Stones, *An Introduction to Educational Psychology* (London, Methuen, 1966), p. 45.

Chapter 5

Approaches and Methods

Reference has already been made to the phonic, whole word and sentence methods of teaching reading. They will now be discussed a little further, as part of an examination of all the various methods and approaches that have been, or are being, employed to teach children to read.

ALPHABETIC METHOD

This was a spelling method, whereby children learned the alphabetic names of the letters and then spelt out and learned the words. Since, in addition to the difficulty this presented, the book from which children learned to read for much of the nineteenth century was the Bible, the modern infant teacher may flinch at the thought of this formidable task. It need hardly be added that this method has long since disappeared!

PHONIC METHOD

The phonic method is based on word building according to the *sounds* of the letters and letter combinations, as opposed to their alphabetic names. It began to replace the alphabetic method in our schools something over a century ago and held sway until it declined in popularity thirty or forty years ago and finally disappeared as an initial method of teaching reading in most of our infant schools. It has since revived, in rather different form, in various approaches which are essentially based on phonic analysis, and these will be examined in greater detail in the next chapter.

The overwhelming disadvantages of the early phonic method of teaching reading were:

(i) The inconsistency of English spelling. Exclusively phonic methods do not help children to read irregularly spelt words.

(ii) The suffocating boredom and irrelevance of reading material restricted to the limited number of sounds a child has learned.

(iii) The lack of distinguishing features in the short, phonically regular words in which only a few letter/sound combinations can be used in the initial stages of learning to read.

(iv) The 'phonic drill', which, though not inherent in the method, was regarded as an essential part of teaching reading at a time when teaching generally was extremely formal.

It was partly because these disadvantages eventually came to be recognised, and partly because formal methods gave way in the 1930s and 1940s to techniques which were based on a strongly child-centred approach to infant teaching generally that the phonic method of teaching reading fell into disuse. Its shortcomings as an exclusive reading method and its association with the rigid attitudes which were being discarded ensured that no part of it could be assimilated into the more informal ideas.

WHOLE WORD METHOD

Gestalt theories of psychology put forward the view that things were perceived in wholes rather than in parts of a whole and so it was believed that children would recognise words as wholes before they could break them down into smaller parts. It was therefore natural that the whole word method of 'look-and-say' should supplant the phonic method. It was theoretically convincing as a way of teaching reading, and the way in which the material could be presented was far more appropriate to the active child-centred classroom than the 'formal drilling' of the bad old phonic days.

One of the main problems which arose, however, was that the child had to know every word before he could read it.

He could not make use of any self-help by building even simple phonic words; for indeed among the extreme supporters of the whole word method any overt reference to phonics, at least before the last year of the infant school, was regarded as pedagogically disgraceful and could not be countenanced. Many teachers, however, surreptitiously applied a little phonic prod now and then; and those who, while appreciating the virtues of look-and-say, were allowed to admit that there were a good many phonic words in the English language and to recognise that many children were quite capable of simple word building long before they were promoted to the senior rank of 'top infant', openly used 'mixed methods'.

MIXED METHODS

These were advocated as early as 1922 in the manual of the *Beacon Reading Scheme* published by Ginn. Its authors believed that children should learn to read by both phonic and look-and-say methods, uniting the two after they had made a start with each approach separately and were in due course ready to use both simultaneously. Schonell's *Happy Venture* reading scheme, published in 1937, renewed the mixed method approach but without the initial separation of phonic and whole word, as in *Beacon*. Simple regular words were first introduced in the text by look-and-say, and when children became familiar with them they began word-building and this increased as reading advanced. The anti-phonic school, however, continued for some time to rely exclusively upon look-and-say methods.

PHONIC WORD METHOD

Reference has already been made on page 27 to the more analytic phonic approach introduced by Daniels and Diack in the *Royal Road Readers*. Here children were taught to see letters and letter combinations, and to hear their corresponding sounds, *as part of a word*—not separately, in isolation, as the earlier phonic method required. Peters describes the *Royal Road Readers* as a scheme which 'for the first time really integrated an analytic approach with a progressive and excellently planned phonic system.'[1]

It is, however, only in comparatively recent years that real interest has revived in integrating systematic phonic teaching with look-and-say methods; and teachers who use the phonic word approach tend to do so by adapting existing reading material to accommodate it. The current resurgence of interest in helping children to find clues for word recognition, and of introducing appropriate phonic teaching in order that they may not be hindered in reading phonically regular words, is likely to lead to greater emphasis being placed on this kind of approach than has been evident since look-and-say methods first gained the ascendancy.

SENTENCE METHOD

A look-and-say method based on the principle that the sentence or phrase is a more natural unit of recognition for the child than the word, the sentence method generally replaced the whole word method and many schemes based on it were published over the years. How far these were in fact used by teachers as sentence rather than whole word schemes one cannot say; and no look-and-say scheme could make incidental phonic teaching quite impossible, since the inclusion of regular phonic words in written English cannot be avoided. However, systematic phonic teaching really could not be undertaken nor, of course, was it intended that it should.

THE APPROACH USING THE CHILD'S OWN WRITING

One development of the sentence method was the practice whereby the child was encouraged to learn to read, in the initial stages, entirely from his own words which the teacher wrote at his 'dictation' below a picture he had drawn of something that was of interest to him. This followed logically from the belief that thought and communication take place in

[1] Peters, *Trends in Reading Schemes*, p. 5.

sentences and if the sentences could come from the child and reflect his own personal interests and concerns he would be strongly motivated to try to read them. This approach also overcame the problem of the arid and remote nature of some of the sentences in introductory reading books, in which the controlled vocabulary and the need for repetition result in wording quite as absurd as anything to be found in the old-fashioned, wholly phonic reading schemes.

In many infant schools this practice was therefore adopted. The child's words were written below his picture every day, comparisons made with the writings of previous days, the sentences discussed, similar words isolated. Again, it at times came very close to being used, in practice, as a 'whole word' method. However, in its original form any phonic word-building was firmly excluded, in the belief that the child found his clues and any help he needed to develop his own word-building techniques entirely from the context.

Usually no reading scheme was used in addition to this approach, but many different books of the appropriate level were made available to the child as he progressed to the stage of being able to read them. Less frequently a scheme was used in parallel to provide 'check points' on the child's progress.

The use of the child's own writing as the basis for teaching him to read was pioneered by J. H. Jagger, an Inspector of Schools in London. Despite its widespread use, however, and its very evident merits it has not, over the years, proved wholly successful as a basic method of teaching children to read. Moyle puts his finger on the reason for this.

It must be faced . . . that Jagger really considered context a sufficient key to unlock the unknown word. This approach to word recognition is, at best, intelligent guesswork and at worst sheer invention. However much we would like to think of reading as thinking inspired by communication through the printed word, we must acknowledge that children can only achieve fluency and confidence in reading if they have some facility in word building. Further, any method in which the child provides his own material brings its own difficulties. The teacher will be heavily taxed if she is to ensure a regular growth pattern in the child's attainment, for the vocabulary will lack control and the repetition rate necessary for memorisation will be difficult to achieve.[2]

However, the practice of the teacher writing the child's own words under his picture continues, and for very good reasons. These are in part connected with providing the child with some of the necessary foundation for reading, such as showing him what words are, that they represent his spoken language, that they are written—and must be read—from left to right, and so on. But the teacher also does this in order to help the child to learn to write, and this will be discussed in more detail in Chapter 10. However, as a method of teaching children to read, to the exclusion or even limitation of other methods, it no longer finds wholehearted support in modern studies of the teaching of reading.

THE LANGUAGE-EXPERIENCE APPROACH

The use of children's own writing as part of their programme of learning to read has, however, recently returned to the scene in a slightly different form and has been given the name of the 'language-experience approach'. Just as Jagger over forty years ago expressed the view that children's own words, in written form, provided the most valuable material from which they could learn to read, so the modern supporters of the language-experience approach attach great importance to the use of the child's language, inspired by his own activities, as the foundation on which his reading programme should be built. The approach has been defined as 'one in which the ideas born of intense interest of a child or a group of children are used as the material for reading. The interest-inspired ideas are stimulated by real or vicarious experiences. These experiences are then recorded to become the written material for reading. Reading, then, becomes part of an integrated language-arts plan.'[3]

Basically many of the common practices, of which infant teachers have for years made extensive use, have reflected the

---

[2] Moyle, *The Teaching of Reading*, p. 34.
[3] Hazel Horn-Carroll (Dallas, Texas), 'The Language-Experience Approach', in Daniels (ed.), *Reading: Problems and Perspectives*, p. 149.

language-experience approach. The captions and the writings beneath children's pictures described earlier; class and individual 'news' books, magazines or diaries; the writing that arises from projects, visits and other experiences; class, group and individual discussions which encourage children to use language, some of which will emerge in written form for them to read—all these activities which result in reading and writing based on children's own interests are founded on the language-experience approach even though they were not in the past accorded the precise title.

Some exponents of this approach seem to support the integration within such a programme of a more structured development of the skills required in word recognition, others do not. The argument appears to have aroused more interest on the other side of the Atlantic, no doubt for the reason that the use of the child's own writing, in one form or another, is already deeply rooted in this country.

However, there may well be room in much of our own practice for making more direct connections between a child's own language and the materials and techniques which we use to teach him to read. This may be particularly true of our methods once reading skill begins to advance beyond the initial stage. A concise and helpful summary of the value, and the limitations, of this approach is given in the opening chapter of *Modern Innovations in the Teaching of Reading* by Donald and Louise M. Moyle, who conclude that 'for the greater success, the marriage of this approach to some more structural type of learning, say a linguistic approach, could draw together the best of both worlds during the early stages of reading development'.[4]

THE USES AND LIMITATIONS OF A READING SCHEME

A reading scheme is not universally accepted as being an essential requirement in teaching children to read. Reading schemes or 'primers' have, however, been used continuously for at least a century in the majority of infant schools and it

[4] London, U.L.P. for the U.K.R.A., 1971, pp. 11–12.

is probably true to say that even today a scheme, or sometimes books from several schemes, are commonly found where children in school are learning to read. It is therefore worth asking ourselves why we so frequently make use of such materials.

The most important reason is probably that a reading scheme provides the teacher with a continuous line of structured or semi-structured learning against which she can measure the reading progress of the children she is teaching. Without such a line of measurement it is much more difficult for her to be sure that systematic progress is being maintained, and it is also more difficult for her to feel confident that reading material is necessarily available to every child at the appropriate level to match his developing skill. With a reading scheme she knows that at least in one area of the reading programme the children can move forward in progressively graded steps. In addition, some teachers believe that reading schemes have value in giving children a goal, and a sense of achievement as they complete one book and set out upon the next. Furthermore, the controlled vocabulary of a reading scheme ensures that a child will always meet many familiar words when he embarks upon a new book and this helps him to feel confident that he is really learning to read. Teachers do, of course, see that the children have a good deal of other material in addition to the reading scheme.

Reading schemes, however, have their limitations. One of the main criticisms of many schemes is that the language and subject matter are so far removed from the everyday lives of most children. The characters and their activities are frequently so depressingly uninspiring and the content of the books is seldom rescued even by the fantasy in which the young child can find so much pleasure. It is therefore very difficult for children to be able to identify themselves with the characters and events, and the motivation of interest and personal concern is lacking. However, it must be added that this complaint is much more justified in some schemes than in others, and there are one or two notable exceptions which are well worth considering from this point of view.

Other criticisms of many reading schemes and their use are that in the early books the limitations imposed by the controlled vocabulary leave no room for anything other than uninspired repetitive wording; that to be tied to a scheme imposes an unwelcome restriction on the child's horizons; that children are inclined to look upon only these books as 'reading' and therefore attach insufficient value to other books; that they can become dominated by the objective of reaching the last book in the scheme, when they then believe that they can read and no further effort is necessary; that with a scheme children can measure their progress against each other and the slower readers become discouraged because everyone else can see they are falling behind; and that once a school is equipped with a scheme, it may be years before there is enough money to replace it if a better scheme comes on the maket. For this same reason teachers have, in fact, little or no choice about the scheme with which they teach.

All these criticisms are valid to a greater or lesser degree, though the effects of some of them can be mitigated by the way in which the teacher uses the scheme and the attitudes she encourages in the children. Some schools try to overcome these problems by having more than one scheme running parallel, using a limited number of books from each. Others use no scheme as a foundation and rely entirely upon children's own writing augmented by a variety of carefully selected books at the correct levels of difficulty.

This has a good deal to commend it, but it would be unrealistic to underestimate the difficulties it presents. The teacher must have a very accurate understanding of the stage of intellectual growth of each child in her class in order to be sure that his reading material is appropriately progressive. She must keep extremely careful records, to be certain that every child at some time reads the kind of book he should be reading at his stage. She must ensure that without a controlled vocabulary the child's confidence is not submerged under the weight of too many new words which he meets in too many different contexts. And she must have very considerable powers of organisation if, with a large class, the pitfalls really are to be avoided. It may be partly because of these enormous demands that reading schemes remain in use and are still found to be of practical help when children are learning to read.

CRITERIA FOR JUDGING READING SCHEMES

Although financial and other considerations in a school rarely make it possible for a teacher to choose her reading scheme, occasionally she does have the opportunity to do so. In any case it is helpful for her to have certain criteria by which to judge the suitability of a scheme for her class. This may enable her to go some way towards compensating for its shortcomings, to modify its application, where possible, according to her judgement, and to extract the maximum value from it. A summary is therefore given in Appendix A of the points that should be considered in assessing the suitability of a scheme.

In order to judge the relative merits of reading schemes and to make comparisons between them, there is really no substitute for a teacher seeing them. Fortunately this is becoming a little easier nowadays. Some teachers' centres, and reading centres, hold a range for teachers to examine at their leisure and publishers will always send inspection copies to a school on request.

A selection of reading schemes is listed in Appendix B, with the name of the publisher, the date of publication, and a comment. This may help teachers to make an initial selection of schemes they would like to see, in order that they may themselves arrive at a considered judgement of the one most suitable for the children they are teaching.

Chapter 6

Learning through Different Media

THE INITIAL TEACHING ALPHABET

One of the fundamental problems facing children learning to read has always been that in written English there are both regular and irregular words. A phonic approach, once the child has made a start, enables him to decode the regular words; but for the irregular words something different is needed. This requirement complicates the early establishment of an efficient decoding system, and also of an encoding system which children need in order to express themselves in writing.

The initial teaching alphabet was devised and introduced for the express purpose of trying to overcome this problem. The aim of its inventor, Sir James Pitman (1959), was to achieve as far as possible consistency between sounds and their written symbols, and the forty-four written symbols of i.t.a. do, in fact, come very close to reaching this objective. The twenty-six written symbols of t.o. (traditional orthography), on the other hand, have a consistency rate with sounds of only about 40 per cent to 50 per cent.

One of the criticisms commonly levelled against i.t.a. is that its forty-four symbols are far too many for the young child to learn. However, a direct comparison between this number and the twenty-six of t.o. is false. There are in fact far more than twenty-six characters for children to learn in our alphabet. At least sixteen of our letters have a different character in the upper and lower case, and two of them, 'a' and 'g', may have two different forms even in the lower case. The total number of written symbols in t.o. is therefore slightly greater than in i.t.a. where the upper and lower case symbols are identical in form, differing only in size. Whatever else the disadvantages of i.t.a. may be, an excessive number of characters as compared with t.o. is not one of them.

The i.t.a. characters

a	ɑ	æ	aʊ	b	c	ᴄh
<u>a</u>pple	h<u>a</u>rd	<u>a</u>ngel	b<u>a</u>ll	<u>b</u>ed	<u>c</u>at	<u>ch</u>air
d	ɛɛ	e	f	g	h	ie
<u>d</u>og	<u>ee</u>l	<u>e</u>gg	<u>f</u>ish	<u>g</u>irl	<u>h</u>at	t<u>ie</u>
i	j	k	l	m	n	ŋ
<u>i</u>nk	<u>j</u>ug	<u>k</u>ing	<u>l</u>ion	<u>m</u>an	<u>n</u>ut	ri<u>ng</u>
œ	o	ω	ɷ	ou	ɔi	p
b<u>oa</u>t	c<u>o</u>t	b<u>oo</u>k	f<u>oo</u>d	c<u>ow</u>	b<u>oy</u>	<u>p</u>ig
r	ʄ	s	ʃh	ʒ	t	ᴛh
<u>r</u>at	f<u>er</u>n	<u>s</u>ock	<u>sh</u>ip	u<u>s</u>ual	t<u>r</u>ee	pa<u>th</u>
ᴛh	ue	u	v	w	wh	y
fa<u>th</u>er	t<u>u</u>be	c<u>u</u>p	<u>v</u>an	<u>w</u>ig	<u>wh</u>ip	<u>y</u>ellow
z	ʒ					
<u>z</u>oo	dai<u>s</u>y					

i.t.a. does not represent a different 'method' of teaching reading. It is neither more nor less than a simplified alphabet. It can be used with phonic or look-and-say methods or both, and though there is not absolute consistency between sounds and their visual patterns the correspondence is very high and this gives the child a much more uniform method of decoding new words than is possible with t.o. It has in consequence been reported that teachers find themselves introducing phonic teaching earlier and more systematically with i.t.a., because the generally consistent sight/sound relationship leads children quite naturally to make the connections themselves. In fact it is now suggested that i.t.a. is more effective if phonic methods are used.

When it was first introduced, there was a very limited amount of reading material published in i.t.a. and for some time this imposed a restriction on what children could read. Now, however, a far wider range of material is available and though it is not quite as extensive as one would wish the restriction on reading activity is much less severe.

The characters of i.t.a. are so designed that they approximate as closely as possible to their corresponding patterns in t.o., particularly the pattern of the upper half of the symbols. If an adult covers the lower half of a line of print, he will still be able to read most of the words; but if he covers the upper half, very little will be readable. It was therefore thought that if similarity with t.o. patterns were retained in the upper half of the characters, transfer to t.o. in due course would be simplified.

There are also other concessions made with an eye on ease of transfer to t.o. Double letters, for example, are normally retained in i.t.a., though these are not strictly necessary in a consistently simplified alphabet. The two written forms for the identical sound of the 'k' and the hard 'c' are also retained, for the same reason; either 'cot' or 'kot' is accepted from the child when he writes in i.t.a., but the teacher always uses the symbol required in t.o. in order to establish the association which the child must ultimately make.

Many investigations into the effectiveness of i.t.a. have been conducted in recent years and the results to date have been extensively evaluated and publicised. To anyone wholly converted to it as a medium for teaching children to read, its value seems to have been proved beyond doubt. But it has not overwhelmed our infant schools and children learn to read and write without it. Why, if its merits are as outstanding as its supporters claim, has it not replaced all other approaches to the teaching of reading? As in so much else connected with teaching, there is not an easy answer to this question.

Although only some 10 per cent of British primary schools use it, it is claimed that with i.t.a. children learn to read more easily and more quickly, that they will eventually read more efficiently, and that they can learn to express themselves in writing with much less difficulty than they experience with the varied and complicated word patterns they meet in t.o.

The first rigorous investigation into the whole question began in September 1961, with an experimental group of schools in which children learned in i.t.a. and a control group where they learned in t.o. The two groups were carefully matched in order to eliminate, as far as possible, other variables. There was some criticism that, in the event, it proved impossible entirely to exclude other influences which could affect the results (such as the skill of the teacher, the effectiveness of a conscious 'reading drive' and the novelty of new materials in the experimental schools); but on the whole it was felt that though these influences might cause the results to be accepted with some reservations, their effect was not sufficiently marked to invalidate the findings.

The results of the experiment pointed to the following conclusions: [1]

(i) The children in the experimental (i.t.a.) group made significantly faster progress in reading than those in the control (t.o.) group.

(ii) The children who learned to read in i.t.a. were able to read in t.o., when they made the transfer, rather better than the children who had learned in t.o. But their progress was interrupted. They lost ground appreciably during the transition period. It was suggested that this might have been due to faulty methods applied during transition.

(iii) Three years after transition 'the children taught in i.t.a. were significantly ahead of t.o. children on the Neale Reading Test in speed, accuracy and comprehension, in spite of the setback during transition'.

(iv) The results appeared to confirm 'the overall impression that i.t.a. children were genuinely superior in their written work'.

(v) Anticipated spelling difficulties after transition to t.o. did not seem particularly to afflict the i.t.a. children. If anything, their spelling was slightly better than those who had learned in t.o. This might be because the consistency between symbol and sound to which the i.t.a. children were so accustomed 'provided a more precise framework within which to learn spelling rules'.

In 1963, the first experiment was expanded and a second begun. This was intended to check the earlier results, and further steps were taken to minimise the effects of the ex-

---

[1] These conclusions are taken from 'An Evaluation of the Research Report on the British Experiment with i.t.a.' by John E. Merritt, in Daniels (ed.), op. cit., pp. 76–9.

traneous influences which had cast some doubt on the validity of the first investigations. Broadly speaking, the findings of the second experiment confirmed those of the first, though the superiority of the i.t.a. children was this time less marked. Moyle calls their average scores 'slightly superior'. He goes on to say: 'From an experimental point of view it established that i.t.a. has some advantages but a more searching analysis of its use is still required before one could entertain the suggestion that all children should use it.'[2]

An independent evaluation of the experiment was undertaken for the Schools Council by Warburton and Southgate, who reported favourably on the results in 1969. However, contrary to the findings of the first report, they did not find that the i.t.a. children retained their lead in reading after about the third year in school. Southgate suggested that this may be due to a general lack of organised development of reading skills once children have 'learned to read'. 'All that is happening at present is that the i.t.a. children reach this plateau earlier than the t.o. children who, within two or three years, catch up with them. They are then all prevented, through lack of guidance and instruction, from making a continued surge of progress. A somewhat similar picture can be noted with regard to children's free writing.'[3]

Referring to some of his own research, which included an investigation into the question of transfer to t.o., John Downing says:

. . . although my research agrees with Southgate's that there is no noticeable problem at the stage when children make the transition from i.t.a. to t.o., I nevertheless have reservations on this conclusion.

Briefly, although i.t.a. pupils transfer to t.o. with all the outward appearances of an easy facility and no anxiety whatsoever, nonetheless the data from objective reading tests shows quite conclusively that a real setback in the learning curve does occur at this stage. . . .

[2] Moyle, *The Teaching of Reading*, p. 78.
[3] F. W. Warburton and V. Southgate, *Initial Teaching Alphabet: An Independent Evaluation* (London, Chambers & Edinburgh, Murray, 1969), p. 164.

Although the i.t.a. children are found to read t.o. 'at least as well as the t.o. pupils can, they cannot read t.o. as well as they can read i.t.a. and the setback on transfer is inescapable'. Downing believes that further research is needed into the possibility of some modification of i.t.a. which might enable i.t.a. children to maintain their lead when they make the transition. 'My view has been challenged by some of the i.t.a. enthusiasts who seem to regard i.t.a. as so perfect that it should be inscribed on holy tablets which must never be violated.' But 'this issue does not have any relevance for the essential decision of the present moment, that is whether to adopt i.t.a. for classroom use *now*. We don't know if i.t.a. can be improved, but we do know with real certainty that i.t.a. as it is currently constituted is a great improvement on t.o.'[4]

A teacher who is teaching children to read and write through the medium of i.t.a. may feel very convinced of its many virtues—for certainly they are there. She may then move to a school where the medium is t.o., and after all it does not seem so much more difficult to teach children in this way either. We must admit, in the end, that despite all the arguments in favour of i.t.a., it still remains the teaching medium in only a small minority of our schools.

Does this imply a certain innate conservatism and unwillingness to change? It is very doubtful that it does. Primary school teaching methods in this country are far from being noted for conservatism and dedication to well-worn traditions. There are three much more likely explanations. One is that the cost of re-equipping a school to make the change to i.t.a. is considerable and the head teacher and the staff must be very convinced that it is markedly superior to justify the expenditure against the demands of the many other things they would like to have for the school. The second probable explanation is that there is nowadays such a great range of children's literature of real quality that we are very hesitant to exclude some of it from the experience of our youngest children in school because it is not printed in i.t.a. If i.t.a. swept the country then presumably this difficulty would disappear. But it has not happened yet.

[4] Merritt (ed.), *Reading and the Curriculum*, p. 75, paper by John Downing.

The third reason for the apparent unwillingness to adopt i.t.a. may be due to reservations about teaching children to read in an alphabet so different from that which surrounds them in their lives outside school. It is possible that a child may be quite strongly motivated to learn when he finds one day that he can recognise a word in a television caption. This motivation may well be lost, at a very important stage, if he is learning in i.t.a.

Thackray strikes a balanced note in his conclusion when reporting on the results of his own research into readiness for reading with i.t.a. and t.o. He found that children were ready to read earlier and made quicker progress using i.t.a., but he also confirmed the setback during the transfer stage.

If firstly, children learning to read with i.t.a. were taught with confidence at a rather earlier age than is normal for the teaching of reading with t.o. and secondly the transfer to t.o. could be made easier in some way, then i.t.a. children could keep their lead and reading standards could be raised. . . . Although my research shows that after three years children learning to read with i.t.a. had similar mean reading scores to children who have learned to read with t.o., I believe i.t.a. is still worth trying because of the other benefits it brings in its train, the main ones being an improvement in creative writing and increase in confidence on the part of the young learner. i.t.a. is worth trying only if the teacher prefers this medium and believes it will bring results. i.t.a. should not be imposed from above on unwilling schools and unwilling teachers; if it is, it will surely fail.[5]

WORDS IN COLOUR

This was devised in 1962 by Dr Caleb Gattegno of Cuisenaire fame. Like Pitman, he was concerned to reduce the difficulties arising from the complexities of written English which children encounter when they begin learning to read. He sought to do this, not with a different alphabet as in i.t.a., but with a wholly consistent colour code applied to t.o. Every sound, without exception, has its own colour. Learning to read is seen as a process of learning to decode and this takes place in an

[5] D. V. Thackray, 'Readiness for Reading with i.t.a. and t.o.', in Merritt (ed.), op. cit., p. 124.

extremely systematic and clearly defined reading programme. The method employed is phonic—the sounds are decoded according to their colours and are then fused to make the word.

The step-by-step progression is almost mathematically precise. Gattegno believes it to be essential that the child is made responsible for the 'automatic assimilation' of each step and the planned method of presentation is intended to achieve this.

It is our pupils, not we ourselves, who have to learn to read and write. If they are to do this, we must use our knowledge of our own mistakes and failures, to discover their difficulties and to remove obstacles from their path. Delegation of responsibility to the learner, at once, and all the time, is essential. This, we shall see, is translated in practice into letting children discover for themselves; into creating situations where they must do the thinking, without being given clues by the teacher.

The teacher must know what the children need, and must present the material to them in such a way that they can develop their reading and writing skills creatively. 'That part of the skill which cannot be discovered or invented will be given to the learner; after that *he* must do the work and the earlier we hand over the responsibility the better.'[6]

The whole reading programme is contained in Gattegno's materials, wall charts, basic books, worksheets, word and sentence building apparatus, coloured blackboard chalks, a film strip and a book of stories. No other books or materials are meant to be used (though this is in fact not impossible in the later stages of the programme). Forty-seven sounds are identified, and each has its corresponding colour; but the colours are for use only when new sounds are introduced. Once the children know the sound they no longer need the colour and the wall charts then function as an *aide-mémoire*. In their own writing the children use only one colour, having established from the colour code the letters that they need. The progression and method of teaching are minutely detailed, at every stage, and the intention is that the teacher should not deviate from the planned programme at all.

⁶ C. Gattegno, *Words in Colour: Background and Principles* (Reading, Educational Explorers Ltd, 1962), pp. 3–4.

Because it is designed as a complete and very carefully developed reading programme it is essential that the teacher is fully acquainted with it before she embarks upon it with children. She must familiarise herself in advance with all the materials, with Gattegno's principles, and with his intentions and instructions on how the programme should be used. Without this careful self-preparation beforehand, it would hardly be possible for her to do justice to the medium. In this respect it is not very easy for a teacher new to a school where *Words in Colour* is used to accommodate herself to its requirements as she goes along.

Unfortunately the teacher cannot look to much evidence for guidance on the effectiveness of this approach, because too little research has been undertaken in this country to be anything but inconclusive. *Words in Colour* is not very widely used in Britain. There is no accurate information on the number of schools where it has been adopted, though the total is certainly much smaller than those using i.t.a. For these reasons, an objective evaluation of its effectiveness, as compared with other media through which children are taught to read, is hardly possible.

Obvious reservations are that the somewhat mechanistic approach requires a degree of formal group instruction and practice that is alien to many deeply held beliefs in infant teaching; that there is too little opportunity for harnessing the child's own language and experience in introducing him to the printed word; that the content of the three basic books and the other early material is undeniably dull and lifeless; and that the teacher is too closely tied to a reading programme which she cannot integrate into the many other activities which may directly or indirectly contribute to reading success.

On the other hand, it must be said that teachers who are convinced of the value of this approach and who use it successfully would not agree that these reservations are justified. They would argue that the programme is so carefully graded and so systematically structured that the ease with which children learn to decode words outweighs any disadvantageous effects. Until, however, we have more objective evidence than is at present available, we cannot reach a convincing conclusion. We must, like Asquith, wait and see.

COLOUR STORY READING

This represents another attempt to regularise written English, this time by the use of colours and shapes to help in decoding the printed word. It was devised by J. K. Jones and he reported on it in 1967 following a research project in which it had been tested in nineteen primary schools.

Unlike *Words in Colour, Colour Story Reading* does not provide a complete code. Only four colours are used—red, blue, green and black; and some of the black letters and letter groups are superimposed on a background of coloured squares, triangles and circles. The four colours and three shapes therefore provide a fairly large number of permutations to which the different sounds may be attached but, though fairly complete, it still remains only a partial code.

The basic approach is phonic and there is only a limited range of material—three children's books, a wall chart and a kit of illustrations and games. An unusual feature of *Colour Story Reading* is that it is introduced to children by means of nineteen delightful stories for the teacher to read. These are summarised in the children's books. They are also available on three long-playing records.

As an approach it is rather less formal than *Words in Colour* in that the programme is not nearly so firmly structured and other reading materials can be used as well. The characters in the stories are entertaining and adventurous and there is a good deal of scope for games and dramatic play as suggested in the teacher's manual. The three children's books, however, have a total vocabulary of only 121 words, so *Colour Story Reading* cannot at present be regarded as a total reading programme. But it should not be ignored on this account alone; it may well be used to supplement other reading material especially, perhaps, in remedial situations.[7]

[7] For the reader who may be interested in comparing in more detail aspects of colour codes and i.t.a., there is a very helpful appraisal in a paper by Vera Southgate Booth, 'Colour Codes Compared with i.t.a.', in Merritt (ed.), op. cit., pp. 95–109.

There is also an excellent statement about the three media in *Reading— Which Approach?* by Vera Southgate and G. R. Roberts (University of London Press, 1970), pp. 147–92.

Chapter 7

Phonics and Linguistics

Although the old phonic method with its stilted vocabulary and endless drill has long since been discarded as a means of initiating children into the skill of reading, we have seen that phonics in modern form are again being given much greater weight from an early stage of learning to read. It is necessary here to be clear about the difference between what are, in effect, two rather different phonic approaches:

(i) The *synthetic* phonic approach, whereby sounds are isolated and then blended or synthesised to 'build' a word.
(ii) The *analytic* phonic approach, in which a sound is analysed *as part of a word*. (The phonic word approach of Daniels and Diack is analytic.)

The synthetic approach is still regarded as being too abstract to stand alone as an initial teaching method for beginning readers; hence the use of such devices as colour codes and phonic kits and tapes to give visual and auditory assistance to word building procedures. However, once children have begun to read, simple word building using this approach certainly seems to be within their capacity and it enables them to decode phonically regular words.

But long before children can do this, they can make use of a symbol which is part of a word as a means of helping them to identify it. For beginning readers, after all, the immediate hurdle is word recognition. Whatever devices we may use for the development of reading skill once a beginning has been made, the child in the first place has to find ways and means of being able to distinguish one word from another. Irrespective of the method or approach we use, this fundamental

requirement remains. Suppose, for example, we believe in a language-experience approach. We encourage the child to begin interpreting written language in terms of his own interest and experience. He has a kitten, which provides a starting point. He draws a picture of it, beneath which the teacher writes 'my kitten' for the child to copy. On another occasion she may write 'I have a kitten.' In this way the child begins to build up a collection of familiar sight words, not only about his kitten but about other things which interest him as well. However, the point at issue is that before the child can *read* the word 'kitten'—that is to say, before he can isolate and identify the written pattern that represents the word—he must have some means of distinguishing this pattern from all the other written patterns he sees.

When one really considers the nature of the operation one realises that, whatever the approach, word recognition is central to the process of beginning reading. We therefore help the child with clues of many different kinds. One of these clues is an embryonic form of phonics. In the case of 'kitten' the child may use the double letter as one of his first clues. To begin with it will almost certainly not be a strictly phonic clue; it will probably be just a visual clue—the child will remember the *appearance* of the 'tt'. But increasing familiarity with the letter 't' will help him to begin making the association between the sound and the symbol and in due course this association becomes established. However, the child is at this stage simply recognising a word because one of its component parts is familiar to him. We must distinguish between his use of a phonic clue when he sees it as part of a word (analytic) and the very different process of sounding each symbol in an attempt to decode, phonically, the whole word (synthetic). It is the synthetic approach that seems rather too difficult for most children at the beginning of reading.

The outlines of individual letters and letter groups, with or without their sound associations, naturally do not provide children with the only clues they use in word recognition. But these clues do seem to be very significant and the various phonic kits and games that are now on the market are designed to familiarise children with the written symbols that are the component parts of words and with the sounds which these

symbols represent. In the very first stage of learning to read, when children have not even begun to distinguish the outline of one symbol from the outline of another, these phonic aids are not really of much assistance. At this point children need very simple matching apparatus which helps them to recognise that there are similarities and differences in written symbols and to begin making comparisons between their shapes. However, when this foundation has been laid, activities which give children experience of symbol/sound association are certainly of value.

One of these, the Programmed Reading Kit devised by D. H. Stott in 1962, presents a carefully graded series of games and exercises, each of which is designed to fulfil a particular function in the development of phonic skills. Its approach is analytic—in other words it is that of the phonic word method. The material was assembled experimentally in the first place for use with retarded children. Convinced of the value of the phonic principle in the teaching of reading, Stott recognised that reading books restricted to phonically regular words were unavoidably too narrow and artificial in content to appeal to children. He therefore set out to devise a means whereby the basic phonic facts could be presented independently of reading books, and of the Kit he says that this, fundamentally, is its *raison d'être*—'the Kit can be said to be a new approach to the teaching of reading which circumvents the disadvantages of straightforward phonic teaching while maintaining the advantages of the phonic principle.'[1]

Since each step in the Kit is itemised and its function carefully explained in the manual, the teacher who wants to give a group of children practice in some particular phonic skill can extract the appropriate game or exercise and use it, if she wishes, independently of the rest of the programme. Thus the Programmed Reading Kit can be used selectively alongside any method of teaching reading and it is therefore an extremely useful piece of equipment to have in the First School. In addition, there is no doubt of its value with older children who have failed to learn with more conventional materials.

The study of linguistics is the study of the form and structure

[1] D. H. Stott, *Roads to Literacy* (Glasgow, Holmes, 1964), p. 48.

of language, both spoken and written. All languages have a structure and pattern, and all have certain requirements and constraints which limit our choice in the way in which we use language. For example, we have just used the phrase 'All languages have a structure and pattern.' There is only one other way in which the words of this phrase can be acceptably assembled. We can say 'All languages have a pattern and structure;' but we cannot say 'All languages a pattern and structure have.' Similarly, there are constraints on the structure of words. There are only certain letters that can precede or follow other letters. Pronunciation also has rules. The terminal 'e', for example, lengthens the vowel sound, as in 'mane'.

In other words, *there is a system.* The system in English may not be the easiest, and certainly as far as spelling is concerned it is not the most consistent of all languages. However, in our habit of lamenting the lack of consistency in the structure and pronunciation of English words, we are apt to overlook the constraints which exist and the assistance which these constraints give us when we read and write our language.

The linguistic approach to the teaching of reading is one which pays attention to the question of helping children to learn that there is a pattern and ultimately to learn what the pattern is. By helping them to look at the structure of words, we help them to analyse word patterns so that they can use these patterns for decoding (reading) and encoding (writing) other words. By helping them to assemble words in language patterns we help them to operate a system of language structure. Until they can do this they cannot use contextual clues to help them with unknown words when they read, nor can they assemble words fluently when they try to express their thoughts in writing.

For beginning readers, these precise objectives are still some distance away. But the linguists would argue that a linguistic approach enables teachers to develop a reading programme based on the use of language as it is known and can be defined; and as children learn how the 'system' operates they can use this knowledge to help themselves as they develop their reading skills. If they are given the coding system, they are given the means by which they can break the code. Even in laying the foundations with beginning readers, the teacher who is familiar with linguistically valid objectives will help children to look at words, so that in due course they will be able to perceive something of their structure and understand some of the rules.

One of the first exponents of a linguistic approach to the teaching of reading was C. C. Fries, who developed a theory based on the proposition that there are certain basic patterns which must be identified and mastered by children learning to read. He rejects the synthetic phonic approach of 'sounding and blending' for beginning readers in favour of an analytic phonic method which takes account of what he calls 'spelling-patterns'. In his view there are five vowel spelling-patterns which beginning readers need:

(i) *The short vowel pattern*, as in *at, man, cap.* All the short vowels belong to this pattern.

(ii) *The open vowel pattern*, which is the terminal single vowel of a syllable, as in *my, he, so, la*-dy, *du*-ty. The sound is always that of the long vowel.

(iii) *The vowel lengthened by 'e'*, as in *fate, bide, hope.*

(iv) *The double vowel*, as in *seat, coat, food, been.*

(v) *The vowel with an 'r'*, as in *bird, work, farm, burn.*

Fries believed that at a very early stage of learning to read children must develop an accurate and rapid response to spelling-patterns. The first step in this process was to present pairs of capital letters of similar formation and the child would say which pairs were the same and which were different, for example:

I	T
T	T
I	I
T	I

At this stage the letters would not be named. The exercise and the child's response were concerned only with the visual pattern. In due course the child would progress to a comparison of short words, and this was the point at which the sound association was first introduced. The *whole word* was named by the teacher—not the separate sounds of the component letters.

By these graduated steps the child learned to respond to spelling-patterns, which slowly increased in complexity as the responses became established firmly enough to be automatic. This was the first stage of learning to read, which Fries called the 'transfer' stage because the child was simply transferring 'the auditory signs for language signals' (i.e. his speech, which he has already learned) 'to the new visual signs for the same signals'.[2]

Having mastered this transfer stage the child then moved on to the 'productive' stage, when responses were automatic and he would read with understanding. Expression and intonation were then important. Finally he progressed to the 'imaginative' stage, when he would read with judgement and appreciation and for the extension of his own experience.

For the mastery of the transfer stage Fries estimated that between 500 and 1,000 hours of practice would be necessary. He believed that the inclusion of any extraneous motivation, such as interest in 'a story as a story', would only distract the child's attention from the learning task. There was therefore no disadvantage in what many teachers would regard as the barren nature of the early reading material, brought about by the limited range of spelling-patterns which could at that stage be used.

Despite Fries's valuable contribution, as a linguist, to the theoretical study of the teaching of reading the gulf between the practice he proposed and that of reading teachers has never been bridged. Two years later another linguist, Lefevre,[3] expressed disagreement with Fries's emphasis on single words. He favoured an approach much nearer to the sentence method, because he believed that only a sentence or string of words could qualify as a 'meaning-bearing unit'. Single words could be recognised without any meaning being attached to them; only when they were assembled into something like a sentence could meaning really be said to exist. In learning to read, the sentence must therefore be the linguistic unit.

Lefevre's emphasis is thus much more on sentence structure

[2] C. C. Fries, *Linguistics and Reading* (New York, Holt, Rinehart & Winston, 1962), p. 120.
[3] C. A. Lefevre, *Linguistics and the Teaching of Reading* (New York, McGraw-Hill, 1964).

than on the structure of words or the association between sounds and symbols. In his book he identifies the linguistic principles which he believes are essential to successful reading teaching but, unlike Fries, he has so far not developed a programme or method by which he proposes that his principles should be put into practice.

For the teacher of young children grappling with the problem of trying to teach them to read, these linguistic theories may seem rather remote from the reality of the classroom. However, we cannot dismiss the work of the linguists. There *are* patterns in language, it has a certain structure, and it conveys meaning in ways of which linguists are aware and which reading teachers are often criticised by linguists for not appreciating. Moreover, though we accept that word recognition is central to learning to read in the first place, we cannot escape the fact that as reading progresses words do not stand as isolated units, unrelated to each other either in meaning or in language structure. As a child learns to read he must learn to put words together so that he understands the message. This is difficult for him in the beginning because he is concentrating so hard on 'decoding' that the context cannot help him—he may not even remember the word he has just read once he has turned his attention to the next one. If, however, we can present the child's reading material to him so that it is more in accordance with linguistic forms and also with the way in which he uses language (so that the language itself has more meaning for him), then perhaps we may help to modify his reading problem. It is in these areas of teaching reading that there is much to learn from linguistic studies.

The difficulty has been the lack of an effective bridge between the expertise of the linguist and the practical reality of the professional task confronting the reading teacher. However, the application of linguistic principles has now moved much further into the classroom with the work of David Mackay and his colleagues, who have developed a practical linguistic/ language-experience approach to the teaching of reading with the *Breakthrough to Literacy* materials. This approach is based on the belief that the teaching of reading (and writing) must be founded on a sound theory of literacy. Moreover, if children learn to produce written language while they learn to read it, they can use their own language resources to help them in the task of becoming literate. The Teacher's Manual which accompanies the materials identifies the linguistic principles on which the approach is based, and it relates the theory to the practice in a way which cannot be at variance with the beliefs and the experience of the modern reading teacher.

When we came to plan materials for use in the classroom, we set out to provide children with the means whereby they might read *and* write from the beginning of their literacy learning. We were concerned to discover an appropriate way for the children to *produce* written language for themselves as well as providing special texts introducing them to the *reception* of written language. The emphasis we came to place on *production* in the first stages of learning to read is one of the places where we depart from the basic assumptions of traditional teaching methods in this field.[4]

Thus one of the objectives of this approach is to enable children to assemble the words of their own language, in written form, in such a way that by this means they can learn to read and write. Before this can happen, however, they must understand what written language is—which part of the 'picture' in a book, for example, represents the writing as opposed merely to a line of decorative marks which might be there simply to finish off the picture. The manual gives detailed and practical advice on how the teacher can help the child to achieve this understanding.

There is a Magnet Board and a set of figurines which may be attached to it. These are really pre-reading materials which are intended to encourage interest and discussion about everyday as well as imaginative situations. There is a Teacher's Sentence Maker, which consists of a stand, printed inserts containing the most common words which children were found to use, and some blank inserts for additional words. The teacher uses this with a group of children, assembling, with the children's assistance, their own words in short phrases and sentences. The sentences are then written, by the teacher, on a sheet of paper which is preserved for reading and future

[4] Mackay *et al.*, *Breakthrough to Literacy*, p. 91.

reference. The manual points out that all this must be done in very small groups and should be informal and relaxed.

As the children acquire by this means a recognition vocabulary of a certain number of words (the manual suggests twelve), each child is given his own Sentence Maker which again consists of a stand and printed and blank inserts. The child now learns to assemble words himself in his Sentence Maker, and the teacher checks them and writes them out for him to keep. In due course he has a Word Maker in which he assembles the written symbols that make a word. The manual insists that the word 'symbol' rather than 'letter' be introduced from the beginning. 'Shop', for example, has four letters but only three symbols, *sh*, *o* and *p*. Accurate terminology will simplify phonic training. As children progress, the Word Maker is used for assembling the derivatives of words—for example *hop, hops, hopping, hopped*—and for varying the symbols in similar words, such as *in, bin, thin, spin*.

The manual leaves very little to chance. While giving the individual teacher every opportunity to use her own ideas it provides her with a well structured framework for the children's language development. It also offers a helpful range of suggestions which take the children through a comprehensive programme of learning to read and write, largely through the medium of *their own language*. It is here where so much of the value of the *Breakthrough* materials lies, and where the expertise of the linguist is so happily married to that of the reading teacher. Mackay gives some examples of sentences composed by 5-year-old Manchester children using the Sentence Maker, which illustrate that there is nothing unrealistic or impractical in his application of linguistic theory to the classroom.

Mummy went to the clinic instead of to school this morning.
We have all been to church to see the font.
We have got a new bath and washbowl and toilet.
Only me is going to Auntie Betty's house.
Diane and me were playing at monsters.

'Such sentences,' adds Mackay, 'show children making use of their own linguistic resources, using the language the way they know the language works and dealing with a wide range of personal interests.'[5]

The materials are completed by a number of delightful *Breakthrough* books for children to read, and nursery rhyme cards with an accompanying record. The Manual concludes with Appendices giving useful notes on English spelling and on the speech sounds of southern British English—material which is extremely helpful to the reading teacher.

Whether or not a teacher were convinced of the value of *Breakthrough to Literacy* as the main programme for teaching children to read and write, she could hardly fail to profit from a study of the linguistic principles explained in the manual and translated by the materials into practical form. For the teacher who does not feel justified in entirely abandoning an established reading programme, there is no reason at all why she should not use the *Breakthrough* materials to supplement it. Their versatility makes such a course perfectly practicable. And for those teachers who lament the lack of a reading scheme which uses language and situations appropriate to children's daily lives, but who on the other hand are hesitant to commit their progress to the uncertainties of a wholly un-structured language-experience approach, *Breakthrough to Literacy* goes a long way towards filling the gap.

As the manual explains, 'reading matter for children should, from the beginning, be linked to their own spoken language. The child's neighbourhood dialect may well be the only re-source he brings to learning to read and write, and to present him with written language unrelated to his spoken language is to cut him off from this.'[6] *Breakthrough* helps the teacher to avoid cutting him off from his natural linguistic resources; but it also offers a firm foundation of structured learning based on clearly defined linguistic principles, while retaining the liveliness and originality of children's own language in the material with which they learn to read and write.

The teacher whose children have reached the stage when spelling begins to have significance often finds herself in-

[5] David Mackay, 'Breakthrough to Literacy', in Merritt (ed.), *Reading and the Curriculum*, p. 231.
[6] Mackay *et al.*, op. cit., p. 3.

volved with conflicting views as to whether or not spelling matters. Really there should be no conflict here, because of course spelling matters. Society requires that the adult shall be literate and if his letter of application for a job contains mistakes he is likely to be severely penalised. The only point at issue is whether the child can learn to spell by a more or less natural and developmental process of self-teaching, or whether spelling is a skill that has to be taught. A good deal of research has been done on this subject and here again there is much to be learned from linguistic studies which isolate and systematise the spelling patterns of our language.

There seems little doubt that for most children spelling patterns do need to be taught; otherwise the spelling of every word must be learned independently, which is both unnecessary and unsatisfactory. The problem remains of applying the research findings in the classroom. Margaret Peters suggests that teachers must explicitly solve it. 'The application of research findings will occur when the attitude of teachers to spelling is more positive, so that the attitude of children themselves to spelling is such that they acquire, from the very beginning, a positive self-image about themselves as good spellers.'[7]

[7] Margaret L. Peters, *Spelling: Caught or Taught?* (London, Routledge & Kegan Paul, 1967), p. 82.

Chapter 8

Learning to Write

Considerably less has been written on the subject of how children learn to write than on how they learn to read, and no doubt one of the reasons is that, except in certain specialised areas, there is not very much research evidence on which to base information about the acquisition and development of writing skills during the First School years. This is not to say that there has not been a great deal going on in the schools in the last twenty years or so, which has brought about the situation described in the Plowden Report as 'perhaps the most dramatic of all the revolutions in English teaching . . . the amount and quality of children's writing'.[1] However, we must honestly admit that most of what we know, or think, about how best we may help young children to learn to write is still largely pragmatic, based on experience and observation—our own and other people's. It is against this background that anyone's thoughts about children learning to write must be evaluated.

Spoken language is acquired by every normal child more or less automatically through contact with his environment. It may sometimes be a very restricted language, but it will serve for him to communicate with his fellows and to conduct his everyday affairs. Written language, however, is something he will not learn simply through exposure to the environment—it is a form of language which he has to be taught.

Written language is subject to more conventions than is the case with speech. The shapes of the written symbols are dictated by convention, the units in which they are assembled to form words are dictated by convention, and so is the direc-

---

[1] Plowden Report, para. 601.

tion in which the words are written. The sequence of letters in any word is usually acceptable in only one form and, as one writer has pointed out, there is no *a priori* reason why one sequence instead of another should have any particular significance for a child. However important or personal the sound of a word may be to him, its written form 'will have meaning for the child only when he has been taught something of the conventions which our society has chosen to operate. The meaning the marks have is not a *necessary* meaning, but an *agreed* one, a conventional one, and until the child has been made privy to our agreements, the written language has no meaning for him.'[2] Moreover, when the child begins to write it is not long before he discovers that some of his familiar speech patterns, though quite admissible in everyday conversation, often become inadmissible when he tries to translate them into writing. He can say 'on Fursdy I was sick' and nobody seems to mind. But when he comes to write it down, 'Fursdy' will not do. For some unaccountable reason people make him write 'Thursday'.

These are among the reasons why written language is so very demanding for many children. When one considers the obstacles which face them, one may marvel that they ever learn to write their language at all.

There are two elements in what is commonly termed 'writing'. There is the technical skill of actually forming letters in recognisable outline and of assembling them into conventional word units with spaces in between (a separation which does not occur in speech) and of keeping these units in reasonably straight lines so that they do not obliterate each other; and the question, ultimately, of separating collections of word units with one of several punctuation marks. Then there is the other aspect of writing which involves original composition—thinking of something to write, finding the words in one's vocabulary, solving the problems of discovering how to write them, and finally of putting them together so that they express one's intention and are intelligible to the writer and to another reader. Which do we do first—teach the child the technical skill, or help him to express his thoughts in a form suitable for

[2] Fraser, *Applied Linguistics and the Teaching of English*, p. 122.

writing in order that he may perceive the reason for learning how to make marks on paper?

The answer probably is that we teach him both elements of writing simultaneously. We begin by giving him activities which are designed to help him to control his pencil and to see how letters and words are formed; and we encourage him to express his thoughts about things which he finds interesting enough to express, and the technical business of writing them down is done for him until he can do it himself. Thereafter we continue in one way or another in this dual role.

For many children the initial technical skill is not so very difficult to master. The really demanding part of writing is that which is concerned with learning to use language in written form. It is often said that children learn to write by writing. This is probably true of the basic skill, in the sense that any such skill needs practice if it is to become effortless and easy to manipulate as a working tool. But to use written language with coherence and clarity and discrimination, to say nothing of such imponderables as taste and originality, surely requires a great deal more than just having the opportunity and the encouragement to write. These, certainly, are very necessary. But the child also needs help in learning *how* to use his language when he writes it, and though this goes far beyond the First School the foundations of this accomplishment are laid while he is there. It is with these foundations and with the bread-and-butter technique of learning how to write words on a piece of paper that we are here essentially concerned.

The first requirement when we consider children learning to write, both in the initial stages and as their skills develop, is the vital matter of their having something to write about. This is closely bound up with learning to read, in which the child's linguistic development plays so central a part. Just as he needs activities and interests which give him something to talk about in order to develop his language skills as a foundation for learning to read, so he needs the same extension of his personal and linguistic experience so that he may have something to write about and the ease of self-expression which the selection of a pattern of written words requires. There is probably little else so certain about teaching children to write than that we have to make sure there is something which concerns them enough to justify the effort of putting pencil to paper.

As children progress through the primary school they may develop writing techniques which vary according to the kind of writing they are doing, for example according to whether they are giving a factual account of the results of an investigation or whether they are writing imaginatively or even just for the purpose of savouring words and finding richness in language. For most of the First School years, however, these distinctions do not arise. The child is simply learning to write his language, extending it in all directions at once irrespective of the nature of his subject. This is not to say that some young children are not more imaginative than others, that some do not take greater pleasure in searching out words which satisfy them, that some are not more interested in expressions of fantasy while others prefer to make more factual accounts. These differences can show themselves quite clearly before children leave the First School. But in learning to express their thoughts in writing there is no real distinction in the minds of most young children about the kind of language which is more appropriate to one piece of writing than to another. They just write, and in doing so they give their teachers the opportunity of helping them towards a variety of expression which, in its lack of contrivance, does not suffer from stylistic restrictions which young children cannot yet accommodate.

'Having something to write about' is a requirement which is frequently admitted but not so frequently met. While we may agree that some children, some of the time, are not at a loss for ideas which justify the effort of expressing them on paper, we must also accept that the global injunction to 'write your news' or 'write a story' or even 'write something about Red Indians' because this is the current topic will all too often be unproductive of any but the most arid result. Children just do not have momentous bits of news every day, nor are their minds for ever overflowing with ideas for stories or even with coherent thoughts about Red Indians that can hardly wait to be written down.

The pendulum of opinion swings back and forth. Giving children something to write about used to begin with 'news', progressing to topics and story cards. One now detects that 'experience' is the thing—that nothing a child writes about is worth anything at all unless it has arisen from an experience in his rich learning environment. While in no way wishing to diminish the value of experience, we are surely not justified in restricting a child's written language only to that which can be directly attributed to his 'discoveries' or to his fascinating experience in the sandpit. The indirect effects of all his experience should, one hopes, help him in many different ways. If one of these ways is to give him the confidence and the interest —and the language—to make up a story about a monster with three heads, are we really to believe that such a subject must be disallowed because we have not experienced any monsters lately?

The point at issue is that in giving children something to write about we must not force upon them artificial and unnecessary restraints. Neither must we, on the other hand, go to the opposite extreme of failing to define ideas for writing so that we impose upon all children the impossible task of assembling all their thoughts from scratch, without any help or guidance. Lewis writes, with great truth:

> No one can doubt that a free choice of theme is a powerful incentive for a child in getting him to want to say something to others as well as he can. But the teacher who, with the best will in the world, tries to give the children completely free choice, sooner or later finds that with some, if not all, he is defeating his own ends.
>
> These are the children who, left to themselves, can think of nothing to write about. They will launch out only if given a fair start. In any case, a routine of spontaneity is not only logically absurd; in practice it stultifies itself by remaining a routine. It is not likely that every child will feel the urge to write about something every Thursday morning.[3]

The teacher, then, has a responsibility to ensure that children really do have something which gives them a reason for writing. This is one of the requirements of teaching. The next requirement is in two parts. These two parts overlap, and for most of the time are indistinguishable one from the other.

[3] M. M. Lewis, *Language and the Child* (Slough, N.F.E.R., 1969), pp. 104–5.

However, for clarity of presentation, they will here be separated, though we recognise that such a distinct division would not in fact emerge in practice. One part is called, for want of a better term, teaching children the technical skill of writing; and the other is helping them to develop competence, and pleasure, in expressing themselves in the written form of their language for a variety of purposes. The detailed practical application of these teaching requirements will be dealt with later. For the moment we are concerned with some of the rationale behind the practice.

As far as the technical skills are concerned, the teacher's objective must be that each child shall have the opportunity in his First School years to master the basic elements of these skills to the extent that it is within his capacity to do so. Some young children experience real difficulty with the physical act of writing and sometimes this can afflict those whose linguistic and creative ability are not in doubt. They may know what they want to write, they may be able to organise their thoughts so that they can be translated into writing, they may have a sound intellectual grasp of the conventions of presentation, they may be able to spell a good many words or know where to find others which they need—and yet the business of actually transcribing all this into print is so laborious that written language offers neither pleasure nor satisfaction. These children can become very frustrated, and they need extra help and a great deal of encouragement if they are to be successful. There are also children who have difficulty with the technical skill of writing and who in addition are limited in their ability to use language when they write. These children may well need special help for all or most of their school lives.

The majority of children, however, will fairly comfortably master the technical skill before they leave the First School. For some this may mean little more than that they can copy the printed word legibly and without too much effort. Others will reach the stage of having perfected the skill to the point when it becomes just a tool that can be handled with ease as a means of recording whatever they want to write.[4]

[4] For some helpful practical comments on handwriting, including different styles, see Joan Dean, *Reading, Writing and Talking* (London, Black, 1968), Appendix I.

Few generalisations are appropriate where such a range of attainment is apparent, but certainly every child in the First School should be helped to reach the standard of production in his written work that is compatible with his ability. If he is capable of writing legibly, he should write legibly. If he recognises that in writing words are separated by spaces, his written words should be separated by spaces. If he is able to build simple phonic words, he should do so in his writing without asking the teacher. If he can learn how to spell short irregular words, he should learn them and use them when he writes. He will need direct and straightforward teaching in how to do all these things, and opportunities for practice. If the teacher denies him these benefits she denies him the use of the working tool without which he cannot effectively write.

This does not mean that the teacher attaches so much importance to the perfection of technical skills that the child's use of written language is inhibited. Few teachers of young children today would fall into this trap, and there is no need to put up warning notices. On the other hand, in our anxiety to encourage children to express themselves in writing, unhampered by the restraints of technical perfection which were demanded long ago, we have sometimes lost sight of the fact that fluency and the imaginative use of language are positively hindered until thoughts can be transcribed without undue effort. Technical skills *are* important, in so far as they are a means to an end. Without the means, the end can represent to the child an intolerable labour. This is very different from treating the means as an end in itself.

In expressing himself in writing, the child is likely to go through quite recognisable stages. At first he will make no distinction between spoken and written language. He will try to write exactly as he speaks. This will lead him into difficulty, because in speech we use a great many extra words and phrases which we do not need when we are writing. Ask any adult to describe an event and note all the extraneous odds and ends of speech with which we commonly intersperse our descriptions—'Well, you see . . . I believe there were three, no, wait a minute . . . yes, I think there were four . . . that's right . . . and then, somehow or other . . . well, you know what I mean. . . .' The young child's description of people or events or something he has done contains just as many extraneous phrases, all of which he could not possibly write down even if he wanted to. So he learns to compromise; he writes as he talks, but he leaves out the conversational incidentals. However, it is not easy for him to reorganise his speech into a form of words which is suitable for writing and he needs a great deal of help from his teacher in reaching this compromise.

His next stage is to write the barest of statements, shorn of all possible frills—'I saw a dog' (partly because at this stage the effort of writing is so prodigious that only a minimal collection of words is manageable). Then, as writing becomes easier, we may find several short statements, all joined by 'and'. The transition from these beginnings to the kind of writing which many young children produce towards the top of the First School represents one of the biggest steps in learning to use written language that children will ever take in the same length of time.

This transition requires that in expressing his thoughts the child shall learn to reorganise them from a form which is suitable for speech into one which is suitable for writing; that he shall cultivate the ability to assemble phrases and sentences in his mind and remember them until he can write them down; that he shall select, sometimes from a number of possible alternatives, just the words he wants; that he shall be inventive or descriptive or factually accurate; that he shall make judgements, which some of his subject matter will require; and that he shall assemble all this sufficiently legibly and coherently to be read by him or anyone else and to give him personal satisfaction.

The step is indeed a large one, and let no one imagine that children can take it without the help of intelligent and sensitive teaching. The progress they make in learning to write will reflect as much the quality of teaching they receive as it reflects their own skills and abilities. Learning to express themselves in writing has been described as 'the most difficult achievement that we demand of children. The whole business of translating from "inner speech" to writing is one of extreme complexity, and it is not surprising that so many of our pupils experience difficulties.'[5] Probably no teacher is ever as success-

[5] Fraser, op. cit., p. 123.

ful with every child as she would like to be. But she will be more successful if she is not tempted to believe that, given the experience and the motivation, the child will 'discover how to write'. He will not discover how to write. He will only learn to do so if his teacher teaches him.

Chapter 9

General Classroom Practice and Organisation

In Chapters 10 to 13 the practical teaching of reading and writing at various stages in the First School is discussed at some length. There are, however, a number of general points that are applicable at more than one stage, and to avoid unnecessary repetition these will be dealt with together in this chapter. The detailed application of some of these points is clearly not precisely the same for, say, the pre-reader and the fluent reader; but the variation that will in practice be required is sufficiently apparent to permit them to be considered only once, in fairly general terms.

THE LEARNING ENVIRONMENT

Whatever the stage of development or environmental background of the children, their immediate surroundings in school are of prime importance in creating the atmosphere in which they learn and in which the teacher teaches. The school itself sets the scene in the first place. The entrance hall, the passages and other common areas may be bleakly innocent of visually stimulating material, or they may have attractive displays to which the children have clearly made a major contribution and which are changed at reasonably frequent intervals before the paint has faded and the models have begun to fall apart. The teacher-produced display has a place as well; but it should not be overdone. The beautifully made 'corn dollies' against a background of yellow drapery surrounded by poems in best italic can transform a dull Victorian entrance and can fulfil the very important function of making children aware of high standards of taste, skill and presentation, which one hopes they will unconsciously assimilate. But these displays can also become depressingly artificial if they are given permanent pride of place, and this is something which has to be well considered.

The same applies to the dragon that was the pride and joy of Class 6 at the beginning of last term, but which has now lost its fire and needs to depart for wherever it is that old dragons go. Displays, however, particularly those which have come mainly from the children, do delight and stimulate them; and the teacher will be rewarded for giving them some of her attention and for helping to make the school look like a place where interesting things happen and where children learn with pleasure and purpose.

Most of the children's time, however, is spent in their teaching areas. These may be classrooms or parts of an open plan design, but it is here where the teacher creates the immediate learning environment. Again to avoid tedious repetition the word 'classroom' will be used throughout in a general sense. It would be impossible to keep repeating 'classroom or open plan area', so 'classroom' will once and for all be used to describe that part (or those parts) of the school in which the individual teacher is responsible for providing and maintaining the materials and the background of teaching for the children with whom she is personally concerned.

When children first come to school, reading and writing are not connected only with books; but books are vital all the same, at the beginning and all the way through. We have already given some attention to the importance of experience, discussion, activity and other familiar happenings which play so great a part in laying the foundations of reading and writing skills, but the value of the book as a source of pleasure and as a stimulus to the child's curiosity to know how to read what is in it cannot be overestimated.

Whatever the limitations of the classroom, the designation of at least one part of it as the 'library' area should therefore be given the highest possible priority. Ideally there should be space enough to accommodate the kind of book rack that allows the fronts of the books to be visible; for a few books to stand alone and invite attention; and for a little table and some chairs where children may relax and savour the pleasure of good books, attractively produced and maintained in a good standard of repair. A piece of carpet and perhaps a painting on the wall above add a note of luxury and desirability in a little bit of the room where atmosphere is important. Old and battered books which date from bygone book corners or disused reading schemes do not belong here—in fact, they do not belong anywhere in the classroom. The library area should be an area of taste and quality. The books must be worth looking at and worth reading. They must be the kind of books which invite, and reward, the child's attention. Schools cannot usually provide as many of them as the teacher would like but fortunately the school is not nowadays the only source of supply. The school library service is generally excellent for augmenting the books available and for making possible greater variety and more frequent change than school funds can normally allow.

We have to recognise that by no means all classrooms are spacious enough to accommodate as desirable a library area as we should all like to see. As with everything else in cramped conditions, the best that can be achieved must suffice. But *some* kind of book corner should be devised if this is in any way possible; if it is quite out of the question the teacher and the children must make do with little groups of books here and there wherever space can be found, though it has to be admitted that this cannot really fulfil the purpose which an inviting library area can serve.

As children's reading progresses, and as they begin to use books as sources of information when following a variety of interests, there is much to be said for displaying and accommodating books in several different areas—for example the nature books near the nature table, the books about boats where the 'boat topic' is being developed and assembled, and so on. If such an arrangement is possible it has the merit of avoiding overcrowding in the main library area, and by bringing together children who are following similar interests it encourages discussion and the interchange of ideas. Once again, however, the extent to which this can be done is largely dependent upon space and an ideal arrangement must unavoidably be modified in accordance with the physical limitations of the room.

Since the extension of the child's experience and the promotion of his interest in a variety of situations and things which he may not have come across before are among the objectives which the teacher seeks to achieve, the inclusion in the classroom of certain carefully considered displays and activities is beneficial. There may, for example, be a display of different textures, which could include contrasting surfaces such as sandpaper, velvet, silk, glass, textured wallpaper, wool, brick, etc. It is not suggested that the teacher should bring all these items, set them up, and leave it at that. There should first be a discussion about the possibility of making such a collection which one hopes would arouse enough interest in some children to encourage them to bring things for it. They should then help to set it up, only a few children at a time so that there can be conversation about the 'feel' of the things they have brought. The teacher should write little cards— 'Anne brought this velvet'; or if the collection is too large for this, just the child's name—'Keith's', 'Sally's'—helps to involve the children personally and gives them a connection with the display. They should then be encouraged to give a verbal or, if they can, sometimes a written description of the contrasts they feel in the different textures, perhaps of other things they make them think of, what some of them might be used for, and so on. Writings and drawings could then be assembled in a class book about the display.

There are two points which are important in connection with such a display. The first is that it is not enough just to say to the children 'Now write about it.' Most children will be hard put to it to decide what on earth to write. The teacher needs to help them with some ideas about the kind of things they might think of when they are writing, and once they begin this quite often leads them to ideas of their own. The second point is that not all children will want to write about every display, nor will they be able to. Those who cannot yet write will gain a great deal from expressing their reactions and ideas verbally, and even when the child has the necessary writing skill, the awful inevitability of having to write about everything too often kills interest in the display and successfully defeats the whole object of the exercise.

To conclude, the learning environment should be one in which interest and stimulation spring from the personal involvement of the children and their active participation in the experiences and materials that are there for them to enjoy. Displays of their own achievements—writing, models, drawings, recording of all kinds—not only show them the results of their efforts but add life and purpose to the surroundings in which they spend their day. The environment provides the background and is a source of ideas which help to give intellectual nourishment. The children cannot learn everything from it; but it sets the scene in which they and the teacher can satisfactorily operate.

CROSSING THE SUBJECT BOUNDARIES

This is hardly distinguishable from the learning environment as a whole but for the sake of clarity it is now developed a little further under a separate heading. It is closely connected not only with the extension of interest but also with the everrecurring importance of discussion—and of having something to discuss.

Much of the experience which helps to promote interest and the growth of language comes from activities which, at first glance, may not seem to have much to do with learning to read and write. But many of these activities do in fact help to foster these very skills. They may include the care of live animals, sowing seeds and watching them grow, collecting things for the nature table (from which a number of themes may develop), making models from junk, clay, papier-mâché, etc., dressing up, drama and movement, painting, making friezes and collages from a great variety of materials—indeed it is difficult to think of any area of learning and activity in the First School classroom which does not present opportunities for the child's intellectual stimulation and the growth of his language. The traffic census taken by the more advanced children or the simple graph about birthdays which the little ones have done may have been undertaken primarily for the development of their mathematical skills; but the discussion and the comparisons and the verbal expression of conclusions which have emerged from these activities have probably contributed as much to the children's linguistic development—and so to their skill in reading and writing—as they have to their mathematics.

Learning to read and write therefore draws heavily upon almost every activity in which the children engage. The teacher needs to be conscious of this, in order that she does not miss opportunities. She can, for example, quite deliberately make use of the investigation that is going on about 'things which sink and things which float' to develop reading and writing skills. For the pre-readers this may take the form of small charts, drawn up after the child has made a practical investigation, and illustrated to give him his word recognition 'clue'. There may also be separate word cards for him to match and 'read'.

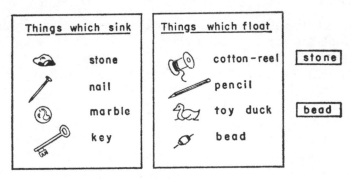

A group discussion about the appearance and sound of the words and any particular characteristics which distinguish one from another would be followed by each child writing and illustrating as many of them as he could. In this way the topic, in addition to its value in other respects, could be used quite consciously to promote early reading and writing skills.

The advanced children would record independently their own further investigations. The teacher could make a few work cards with such questions as: 'Find 3 more things which float and 3 which sink. Why do you think these things floated or sank? Read a book called . . . pages . . . to help you find out.'

Those who are not fluent readers would need something much simpler, for example a sample card showing them how to record what they discover from their activity.

```
┌─────────────────────────┐
│   a _ _ _ _ _ sinks     │
│   a _ _ _ _ _ floats    │
└─────────────────────────┘
```

These children will need to ask for the nouns before they can write them. It is not suggested that they can thereafter read all the words they have used, but like so much reading and writing at this stage the objectives are to introduce them to the vocabulary which arises from interest and investigation, to make apparent the purpose of learning to distinguish the words 'sinks' and 'floats', to give them practice—again with a purpose —in writing, and to arouse their curiosity and interest sufficiently *to motivate them to want to learn.* We do not, of course, exclude other forms of recording their results; a graph, for instance. But we are here particularly concerned with reading and writing skills and the example illustrates a way in which a topic may be used to develop them.

It is because learning arises naturally from a cross-section of subject matter that rigid subject divisions are rapidly disappearing from the programme in primary schools; and this brings us to a matter of principle that is of quite outstanding importance.

In our anxiety to provide a stimulating learning environment because of its value in helping to promote the child's intellectual growth, and in our concern to abolish subject boundaries because almost every area of learning has so much to contribute to every other, we have too often lost sight of *what children are unlikely to learn effectively* from these practices. It is therefore very necessary to try to analyse the situation clearly and honestly, and see what the learning environment and the interdisciplinary approach can do for the child in the First School and what they cannot.

They can do a great deal to inspire in the child the will to learn. They can create for him a rich background of interest in which one intellectual possibility leads to another and one experience presents the opportunity for many more. With the removal of unnecessary subject barriers the child can be helped to perceive the purpose of what he is learning. He finds that some of the activities and investigations that are open to him require particular skills—perhaps to read something or take a measurement or record a result—and the value of reading and recording and measuring is clearer. By having an outlet for his curiosity with pursuits that are within his competence he can gain in confidence and assurance. He can, in short, learn a very great deal by living his school day in surroundings where there is always something worth doing. And as far as reading and writing in particular are concerned he can extend his powers of self expression, he can verbalise about the experience in which he has the opportunity to engage, and in sometimes recording the results of his experience he can be helped to transfer his thoughts to paper.

These are some of the assets that can accrue to the child from the learning environment and from the integration of subject matter as far as it is appropriate to the pursuit of his personal interests. But the child's learning does not end there. However much the environment may contribute and however undifferentiated the subject matter these will not, of themselves, enable him to discover how to recognise words or how to write them. They will not show him how to form letters or to build sounds into words. They will not teach him to interpret print. They will not ensure that his own interests and investigations will present him with reading and writing material appropriate to his level of development. They will not prevent him from being bored and frustrated because he has not yet learned the basic skills that a particular activity requires. And they will not, automatically, make the lazy child industrious or the butterfly apply himself or the really uncertain child make the effort when he lacks the confidence to try.

No one will question that the environment should be rich and varied and should offer the child the intellectual possibilities that he needs to develop his interests and his skills; but it is only when we recognise what the environment *cannot* do that we can use it to real advantage and extract from it the support which it may give to modern teaching methods.

ORGANISATION

The detailed organisation of the children's programme in reading and writing cannot be quite the same if their activities throughout the day are integrated—that is if each child pursues an individual programme which he undertakes in the order of his choice—or if there are differentiated periods of time when all children may be doing, for example, three Rs. The principles governing the organisation of an integrated day or of a differentiated programme, and precise indications of how each may be undertaken in practice, involve a range of considerations far beyond those which can be included in a book about reading and writing; but there are nevertheless certain basic elements which apply in any form of organisation, and it is with these that we are now concerned.

The first essential is that the teacher should, quite deliberately, define the activities and experiences she thinks each child needs at any given point of time. She will almost certainly find, even in a family grouped class with a wide age range, that several children have broadly the same requirements. For example, there is the group of pre-readers. Although one or two may need a little more of this or a little less of that, the activities and materials appropriate to their needs are not very dissimilar. They need word and picture matching apparatus, the opportunity to talk about the shapes and outlines of words, conversational help with recognition clues, the occasion to look at books, the kind of activities which help to extend their experience and the opportunity to use language in talking about them, help with left-right orientation, writing or drawing activities which develop pencil control, and so on; the list is not complete, but it will suffice for the present purpose.

Similar lists can be drawn up for the children at other levels of development, and the teacher's objectives are then defined in terms of the kind of activity and experience she will try to provide for each group, and the materials that will be required. She does not, of course, aim to cover all these things every day but she knows what kind of activities she wants the children to engage in until they move towards the next stage. It is her knowledge of their learning needs and her deliberate definition of what these will entail which form the basis of the daily group or individual programmes.

Having determined upon the nature of the activities which individuals or groups of children need, she must then devise some means of transmitting to them the outline of what she wants them to try to accomplish. With a differentiated programme this is not difficult—the teacher can tell each group or in some cases individual children what she wants them to do. But she cannot do this with an integrated day, so she may make the day's objectives known by calling the children together first thing in the morning to let them know what she expects; or she may work out for each child an individual programme which he understands and which goes on more or less continuously. The detailed means she employs to make the children's objectives known to them will partly depend upon the level of development of the children in her class. If they can read, a written programme will serve; if they cannot, the teacher must tell them. If the children are capable and confident, she can give them their objectives for the whole day —or even longer; if they are very young or uncertain of themselves or of limited capacity she will have to break the programme into much smaller units.

There really is no necessity for programmes or objectives such as these to be constricting or deadening. If they are carefully devised and flexibly administered there is absolutely no reason why children's personal interests or spontaneous investigations should not be given ample opportunity to flourish. But it is illusory to suppose that without objectives, anticipated by the teacher and fulfilled or modified as the day proceeds, children can organise and sustain their own lines of progress and make all their own decisions about selecting the learning situations on which their reading and writing depend.

Having defined the objectives for the children, the teacher's organisational arrangements must then include provision for a number of detailed contingencies:

(i) When a child has gone as far as he can with an activity, what does he do with the result of it, assuming it is of a kind that has a tangible result? Does he hand it to the teacher, or does he put it in a 'marking box'? What measures does the teacher take to ensure that some discussion about the activity can sometimes take place?

(ii) What arrangements are there for a child to move from one activity to the next? Does he really know, for certain, what the arrangement is? (Even if he does know, he will not necessarily conform. But one can always try to train him to do so most of the time!)

(iii) Can the change of activity be sufficiently frequent? A beginner in school is hardly likely to continue at one activity for more than about ten or fifteen minutes—sometimes much less; a more advanced child will go on longer. To insist upon a continuation when the child's span of concentration has run out will be totally unprofitable.

(iv) What arrangements are made for periods of direct teaching of a new process to a child or group of children? Such arrangements are essential and must be allowed for.

(v) If the activities of one group of children need a good deal of the teacher's attention, are all the rest engaged on something which they can manage without very much help?

(vi) What provision is there for children who have finished early or who have 'run out of steam' ten minutes before the lunch break? (Some ideas for 'odd minute' activities are included in the following chapters.)

(vii) Do the children know where to find the incidental materials or help they need for a particular activity?—words for personal writing (dictionaries, wall charts, etc.), the box of letters for word building, the tracing paper and other items of this kind.

These questions all present situations for which the teacher must make provision in advance. They are not peculiar to reading and writing activities; but these activities, as much as any others, require that the answers shall be clear. Without them the teacher will not be able to rely on the support of her organisation to meet the learning needs of the children in her class.

Although there is still a place for the occasional use of class teaching, the group or individual approach has, for reasons known to us all, generally replaced it for most of the day. If a child is to work at his own pace there has to be some means of presenting to him personally the activity or material which has been designed for his particular stage of learning. Organisationally it is not possible for the teacher to do this on a one-to-one basis with every child all the time. Some means is therefore necessary for the independent presentation to the child of some of his learning situations.

One way of achieving this, which is widely practised, is through the medium of card apparatus or assignment cards of one kind or another. The intelligent use of such material can be a help in class organisation, though of course it has its limitations; and not all teachers find it equally valuable. Others, on the other hand, use it extensively. Some of the apparatus which they make—and it is a very time-consuming task if it is well done—can be bought commercially, and if this is possible there is no merit in the teacher spending a great deal of time in making it herself. However, there are always far more demands upon school funds than they can possibly meet and if the choice lies between spending the money on equipment which the teacher cannot very well make or on apparatus she could produce herself, she is likely to choose the former. This is one of the reasons why many teachers make a great deal of the reading and writing material their children use; and another is that the teacher's own material can be personally designed for the needs of individual children in her class whereas commercially produced apparatus cannot always meet such detailed personal requirements.

For these reasons 'home-made' apparatus will figure largely in the following chapters. Teachers who do not want it will not make it; but the suggestions may be helpful to those who do. If they use it, however, there are certain considerations which, if taken into account, can make it more effective and more of a help in terms of organisation.

In the first place, all basic card apparatus designed to help children to learn to read and write must be carefully graded. Moreover, the system of grading must be known not only to the teacher but also to the child. If it is not, then the teacher must personally direct each child to every piece of apparatus he uses or he may find himself in possession of something which is unsuited to his level of development. Either way, this is a waste of the teacher's or the child's time. A clear grading system is therefore essential, and most particularly if an integrated day is in operation and most children are following individual programmes and helping themselves to materials which they are using at different times throughout the day.[1]

A second requirement is that the apparatus should be stored in such a way that it is easily accessible to the children. Ideally, this should be in wall pockets placed at child height, but if lack of space makes this impossible the boxes or cupboards where it is kept should be clearly marked with a coloured strip or symbol or some means by which the children can identify the material they should use.[2]

Card apparatus can all too easily become an educational straitjacket which restricts a child's interest and progress instead of providing him with *one* means of learning tailored to his individual need. If it does become a straitjacket then the teacher has misunderstood its purpose. The purpose of reading and writing apparatus should therefore be examined and an evaluation made of its merits and its possible misuse.

Its purpose is to provide children with a particular kind of material which, in the main, is designed to achieve one of three objectives:

(i) *To help the child to learn a certain skill.* The pre-reader who is using word-matching apparatus is learning to look for similarities and differences between one word and another, and also to look for clues which will help him in word recognition. The child who has a good vocabulary and can write quite fluently but who cannot think of anything to write about uses a story card to give him an idea so that he may go on learning to express himself in writing. A great deal of good apparatus provided for young children comes under this heading.

(ii) *To give the child practice in the use of a certain skill.* The beginner needs practice in the art of controlling his pencil and of forming letters; so he has the outline of a picture or a word to trace, or a writing card to copy. The more advanced child needs practice in word building so he has a card on which there are pictures—a

---

[1] For details of a grading system, see Joy Taylor, *Organising and Integrating the Infant Day* (London, Allen & Unwin, 1971), pp. 28–31.

[2] For instructions on how to make manilla wall pockets, see Taylor, ibid., pp. 30–31.

hat, a cup, a hen, a dog, a pin, so that he may make the words. This category of apparatus often overlaps with the first.

(iii) *To give the child a practical instruction, or a suggestion for a line of investigation, which the teacher could give him personally if she had time.* This often arises, especially with the more advanced children, in connection with a theme or topic—as shown in the examples connected with 'things which float and things which sink' described on pages 100–101. This category also has much in common with the first.

If the teacher's card apparatus achieves one or more of these objectives and if it is designed in progressive stages then it will make a constructive contribution towards the organisation of the children's learning programme. If, however, apparatus is just provided in sheer quantity, without reference to precisely what the teacher hopes the children will learn from it (and this is all too easy for the inexperienced teacher who feels under great pressure to keep all the children occupied on known and quantifiable tasks) then two possible dangers can result. One is that much of the children's time will be wasted on useless apparatus from which they are learning little, and the other is that this vast output of cards will be regarded as representing a kind of 'scheme of work' from which no child must diverge irrespective of his personal need or interest. The teacher's apparatus can certainly assist organisation and can provide a valuable thread of progression which ensures that gaps do not go unfilled. But it can be stultifying if it overwhelms the daily activity and if the completion of endless numbers of cards becomes the only or even the main criterion of progress. Like so much else in teaching, it is the balance between extremes that offers the best chance of success.

HEARING READING

One of the popular misconceptions about teaching children to read is that it is necessary and possible for the teacher to hear all of them read every day. If the class is reasonably small, and if the teacher has the assistance of an 'infant helper', and if 'hearing the children read' is taken to mean hearing them read *something* (though not necessarily from their reading books), then no doubt either the teacher or the helper can, for the record, hear every child read every day. But if these 'ifs' are not included it is quite impossible for the teacher to reach such a Utopian target, unless she spends so much time hearing reading that she seriously neglects many of the other things which she should very properly be doing.[3]

However, we must ask ourselves whether this requirement, hallowed as it is by time, really has the value with which it has for so long been credited. It may be that it is less important to hear a child read every day than it is to use the time that can be devoted to the purpose in such a way that it contributes more effectively to the development of his reading skill. This is an aspect of hearing reading which in the past has been given far less attention than the exercise itself.

When children read to the teacher, they make mistakes. The teacher may correct these, having invited the child to consider what the word really is, and having helped him to arrive at the right answer. However, the *nature* of the mistake, rather than the mistake itself, is something to which we should give some attention. Recent research indicates that there is much to be learned from the kind of mistakes children make in oral reading, and that the teacher's reaction to these mistakes is significant in helping the child to make progress.

The case is extremely well presented by Elizabeth Goodacre in her booklet *Hearing Children Read*.[4] 'Thinking more about the child's types of error rather than the sheer number, brings the situation alive not only for the child but also for the teacher. "Hearing" reading becomes less of a ritual and more of a learning situation for both the participants—child and teacher.'

We have seen that in trying to recognise words children make use of certain clues or 'cues' which help them to distinguish one word from another. There are many possible cues, the picture, the shape of the word, the outline of a known letter,

[3] For some suggestions on the practicalities of hearing children read, see Taylor, op. cit., pp. 85–8.
[4] The extracts in this section are all taken from the booklet, to which the reader is recommended for additional valuable information on hearing children read. See Appendix A for details.

the context etc. Goodacre suggests that in using these cues children are selective. They do not use all possible cues every time. They select 'the fewest most useful cues necessary to produce the right or correct guess the first time.' When a child selects the wrong cue or cues, he will misread the word. If the teacher simply substitutes the right word, this does not isolate the faulty cue and help the child to establish a more reliable one. If, however, errors are regarded as 'miscues' rather than mistakes, and the alert teacher recognises the nature of the miscue, she can often give the child much more positive help with his learning. 'This view of oral reading errors implies that children's mistakes are not the result of inattention or laziness but rather a "misreading" of the situation. The teacher "hearing" a child thus becomes a detective, asking themselves why did he say *that*? Why did he not go back and correct *that*?'

If, therefore, the teacher can take the time to engage with the child in this joint exercise of detection, 'hearing reading' assumes a rather different, and much more positive, character. The necessity for the teacher to give the child time and attention when she hears him read, rather than be obliged to ration these severely in order to hear as many children as possible, is further supported in several studies quoted by Goodacre which show the child's apparent need, at times, for spontaneous re-reading. The studies indicate that children may do this either to correct a mistake they have themselves recognised or to consolidate their learning when they have read a passage successfully, and this seems especially apparent with children in the early stages of learning to read. The teacher must therefore use her judgement when hearing reading, in order to try to avoid correcting the child too quickly. In Goodacre's view 'it may be important to let beginning readers do *some* searching and correcting of their errors. What is probably very important in the beginning stages is not so much knowing a particular word, as the opportunities to develop strategies for figuring out any word. . . . Goodman (1970) found in her study that if encouraged to re-read, three times out of four, children supplied the correct word.' Again, this approach takes time, which cannot be given if the teacher's first priority is to hear as many children read as possible in the course of the day.

Another aspect of children's oral reading which has been

the subject of some investigation concerns, in effect, the familiar phenomenon of 'barking at print'. Goodacre draws our attention to the fact that in spoken language words follow one another without a break, whereas in written language they are separated by spaces. When children first encounter these 'word boundaries' they meet something unfamiliar; and in a study by Clay (1966) it was suggested that 'this understanding of what constitutes a word in print takes some time to develop'. In trying to break up their speech patterns so that they correspond with the separated word patterns of written language, children adopt 'a machine-gun like style of reading' as they try to match the spoken to the written word. Often this is accompanied by pointing with a finger. Clay reported a gradual transition from finger-pointing to this strategy of 'voice-pointing' (or 'barking at print' as we have generally called it, with the implication that it inhibits fluency and must not be permitted). Clay suggested, however, that this voice-pointing 'seemed to serve an important function at the beginning stages of reading in that it aided a child in making the one to one correspondence between the printed and the spoken word.' As reading skill develops, however, voice-pointing diminishes.

These studies have important implications in terms of the child's oral reading and of the teacher's role in hearing him. Apart from underlining the importance of making this an occasion for constructive learning rather than a standard ritual, their conclusions lead also to a modification of the view that barking at print represents a faulty reading technique which must be eradicated as soon as possible: it now seems much more probable that this is a stage through which children must pass. Small wonder that teachers have so often found themselves at a loss in trying to prevent their children from engaging in this 'reprehensible' practice!

READING AND TELLING STORIES

It may not be inappropriate to add a final word in this chapter on the relative merits of reading or telling stories—a question on which there is occasionally some controversy. On the one hand, there is the school of thought which holds fast to the view that the teacher should always tell stories to young children rather than read them, because the book sets up something of a barrier on an occasion which essentially should be comfortable and intimate and when the teacher's attention should be given to the children who are gathered round her. She may have illustrations to support her story and she would certainly let the children know that stories come from books which they will soon be able to read for themselves. But if the stories are told, the children will have the benefit which 'story time' has to offer without, it is felt, the book being a distraction.

There is much to be said for this point of view and undoubtedly the well-told story is a source of lasting pleasure to a great many children. However, we must not forget that there are advantages in stories being read from books as well, and these advantages are closely connected with learning to read. When the teacher is reading the children a story she can help to show them very clearly what the act of reading is. She can, at appropriate moments, draw their attention to the fact that the words she is reading are a translation of the print on the paper before her. When she holds up the book to let them see a picture she can occasionally point out the words which describe it, running her finger along the line to show the direction in which she reads.

Naturally it is not suggested that every story time should be turned into a reading lesson or that the pleasure of the story should be constantly interrupted so that the teacher can add an extra teaching prod on every other page. But stories *do* come from books and children should not have the impression that there is no place for books at a time when they listen to stories. If they are to be motivated to want to read books themselves, they should surely experience the pleasure of hearing their contents; and story time is just the right occasion for this pleasure to be theirs. It need in no way be spoiled because the teacher sometimes helps children to realise what she is doing when she reads.

So the plea here is for both the well-told and the well-read story to have their place. Apart from anything else, not all teachers feel capable of telling stories really well every day. Story time is, for a great many children and teachers, one of the most enjoyable parts of the day. It would be a pity to turn it into another ritual when there is something to be gained from presenting stories to children in more than one way.

THE APPLICATION OF THE THEORY

The next four chapters are intended to be practical and directly related to the classroom, and the material in them will be presented under various headings in note form. This is done in order to provide quick references and it is hoped that the inexperienced teacher in particular may find some of the advice and suggestions helpful. These are neither comprehensive nor foolproof, nor are most of them original; even so, they may help new teachers to interpret some of the theory in practical terms.

Although for the sake of clarity the content of these practical chapters is separated according to different levels of development, it is not suggested that any such clear cut separation is evident in practice; neither are reading and writing stages likely to be as much in parallel as the method of presentation in these chapters might imply. A child may, for example, be advancing quite rapidly with his reading, but be experiencing real difficulty with his writing and still in need of some of the help and material suited to an earlier stage. However, the reader will perhaps bear with these problems of presentation and refer to that part of any chapter which may seem the most appropriate for an individual child.

Chapter 10

The Pre-readers in
the Classroom

THE CHILDREN

These children are, generally, those who have just started school, at the age of five or a little younger. They will vary very much in temperament, in achievement, in their level of maturity and in their reaction to starting school; nevertheless, some broad generalisations are possible.

1. They are likely to be highly individualistic, talking and doing things together but really concerned primarily with their own interests and their own affairs. A small group may, for example, play a 'lotto' game together, but rarely will a child be the slightest bit interested in anyone's results but his own. Reading and writing games and activities must therefore take account of this individualistic approach. Any topics or projects will need to be of short duration and involve only a small number of those who, almost by chance, are interested.

2. Though some children will have made a beginning, the real pre-readers will have no notion at all of what reading really means. They are not aware of what a written symbol is, let alone that some are alike and some are not. The least advanced of them may not even recognise similarities and differences in simple pictures.

3. Their span of concentration is very short—anything from a few minutes to perhaps a quarter of an hour. A few may be able to concentrate for a little longer.

4. Most of them need very clear instructions about what they are to do, and a good deal of help and direction in pursuing their activities. If left to make their own decisions about these they may well feel bewildered and insecure. They must therefore be given well-defined tasks or aims. The teacher will

soon identify those children to whom this may not wholly apply.

5. There may be very great differences in their experience and linguistic ability. Discussion with individual children, with small groups, sometimes with the whole class, is vital. Young children do not mentally divide the words of their speech into the conventional units—for example 'breadnbutter' is one word. This will emerge as they begin to write; experience and teaching will familiarise them with word distinctions. (For some children this continues well beyond the pre-reading stage.)

6. A good many of them find pencil control extremely difficult —their motor co-ordination is just not sufficiently developed. It takes time and experience with the right materials before they can produce a recognisable outline.

7. Most of them are very dependent upon a good relationship with their teacher. Most of their effort is made *for her personally*, and for many children learning to read takes a great deal of effort. The teacher's encouragement and goodwill are strong sources of motivation.

OBJECTIVES AND IDEAS FOR READING

Some of these objectives have already been given fairly detailed attention, but for convenience they are included here in summary.

1. Those children who do not yet realise what reading is need positive help in making the connection. The teacher must take every opportunity to point out the words on a page, to show that written words are separated by spaces, to establish the difference between reading and talking, to indicate that English is written from left to right and from the top to the bottom of the page. All this becomes more evident to children once they begin to write.

2. The teacher must try to generate interest in the written word and help children to perceive the value of reading. Clearly this is more necessary for some than for others.

3. Since linguistic development is so important, and most small children are quite unused to initiating subjects for discussion at a given moment, the teacher must be prepared to do this for them when necessary. Some ideas for discussion:

(a) Homes, families, toys, pets, games, holidays—anything to do with the child's personal life.

(b) Visits, trips, nature walks, etc.; but these will be more productive if the teacher suggests a few points before-hand for particular observation, such as 'Collect some different kinds of leaves to show us afterwards', 'Look specially at the cows so that you can tell us about them', 'Try to remember as many things as you can about the fire-engines, the bus-ride' and so on.

(c) Small topics which may interest groups of children, but at this stage are unlikely to involve the whole class. These may be assembled in practical or pictorial form and used as a starting point for discussion. Activities may include pictures cut from magazines, pasted into a scrapbook and given captions by the teacher. Some possible topics are boats, animals, shoes, clothes, games, different ways of moving (walking, running, jumping, cycling, going in cars, aeroplanes, trains, buses), collecting pictures and items characteristic of the present season, displays of various kinds to which the children contribute, a bird table outside the classroom, growing seeds, observing and caring for an animal—in fact, almost anything which does not require prolonged and sustained effort or a feat of imagination which takes children right outside the limits of their experience.

4. As far as written symbols are concerned, matching activities are very basic. The teacher must think of many different ways in which this can be done in order to give children sufficient experience without the boredom of repetition with the same material. Some children may first need experience of the earlier stage (of matching simple pictures) before they can match written symbols.

5. As children encounter written words, the teacher should give incidental and conversational help in looking for visual clues which assist recognition. Many children will find their own clues and they should be encouraged to talk about them— 'How do you know that word is "look"?'

6. If a reading scheme is used the children should be given every opportunity of meeting and becoming familiar with the

words in the introductory book. To find that they can already recognise a few will give them confidence when they begin trying to read it. Certain items of pre-reading apparatus should therefore use these words, though not exclusively. If there is no reading scheme, some of the most common speech words may be included in pre-reading material; their number should be limited and they should be repeated frequently. It is essential that in early material of this kind the child should have a chance of rapid success. McNally and Murray have compiled a useful list of the most used words in English,[1] and these are given in Appendix C.

OBJECTIVES AND IDEAS FOR WRITING

'Writing' encompasses two aspects:

  (i) *Personal writing*, or the assembly of written words for the purpose of self-expression.
 (ii) *The technical skill* of committing pencil to paper, legibly and in accordance with the conventions of written English.

Personal writing
Only the foundations are applicable at this stage. We have to recognise that these children, even when they have something to write about, are quite unable to express their thoughts in a form suitable for writing. The approach (with the Sentence Maker) suggested in *Breakthrough to Literacy*[2] offers one possible solution. Additionally, or alternatively, the teacher acts as the child's 'secretary' and writes for him at his dictation.

This, however, is not as straightforward as it sounds. The theory is that the teacher's efforts have by now brought about a situation in which every child is bursting with experiences he wants to describe in writing. Of course this happens some of the time with some of the children; but others do not have the faintest idea of what to write about, so the teacher must help

[1] J. McNally and W. Murray, *Key Words to Literacy* (London, Schoolmaster Pub. Co., 1962).
[2] Mackay *et al.*

with suggestions. Eventually it is established that David wants his writing to be about the boat he made that morning from junk materials. Something like the following conversation then ensues :

> *David:* I want to write about my boat.
> *Teacher:* What do you want me to write about your boat?
> *David:* Well, about my boat.
> *Teacher:* Yes, about your boat. But what do you want me to write down about your boat?
> *David:* I want you to write down about my boat. There's my boat that I made. It's red. I want you to write about that.

This conversation may go on for some time. David wants to write about his boat; but he can only express himself as he speaks, and his oral expression is not suitable for direct translation into written form. He cannot adapt his speech to a short, coherent sentence for the teacher to transcribe at his dictation. So she must suggest a form of words which will effect the transition from speech to writing.

> *Teacher:* Shall I write 'I made a red boat'?
> *David:* Yes, that's the boat, there on the window-sill.

So the teacher writes 'I made a red boat', saying each word as she writes it and getting David to say each word with her. Ideally, she and David may look back to an earlier piece of his writing, which also happens to include the word 'made'; they look at the word 'red' on the colour chart and make the comparison; they comment on the 't' at the end of 'boat'. Finally David tries to trace or copy the words the teacher has written, and he draws a picture of his boat.

This operation has taken several minutes of the teacher's time; but many vital teaching points have been made:

   (i) David has been helped to assemble words in a form suitable for the expression of his thoughts in writing.

  (ii) He has seen words and letters being formed, his eye following the teacher's pencil along the line from left to right.

(iii) His attention has been drawn to the assembly of written symbols in word units, each unit named and separated by a space from the next one.

(iv) He has had experience of what the written word signifies, and of its connection with reading.

One such experience does not teach David to read and write in a sudden blinding flash of insight; but an accumulation of such experiences unfolds the purpose of these skills and of the techniques they require. The foundation of personal writing is being laid.

If the teacher is to give David the time that is needed for the exercise to be productive, she clearly cannot do this every day for every child unless the class is family-grouped and fairly small, with only about half a dozen children at this initial stage. If many more are in the same position as David, she must split them into groups and apply the technique just described to one group each day so that all have their turn as often as possible. The others must be given something which they can accomplish with less of her attention, such as tracing, copying from writing cards or copying the day's 'news'. It is far more profitable for the child to be given, once in a few days, enough of the teacher's time to assemble his own writing really constructively, than to have a sentence hastily written for him every day, purporting to transcribe his own words but in fact amounting to little else than just something more for him to copy.

The technical skill
The child has two requirements at this stage: the opportunity

(i) to learn how to control a pencil; this is partly a matter of physical development and partly of getting used to it;

(ii) to learn how to make the shapes of outlines with sufficient accuracy for them to be recognisable.

Nothing more than this applies to begin with, but for these requirements three things are necessary:

(i) The use of correct materials—large, plain paper; thick, soft pencils; fat crayons.

(ii) The opportunity to see the shapes of written symbols being made—the teacher's writing in the child's own book, on the blackboard, on the news sheet, etc.

(iii) The opportunity for practice, both in pencil control and in letter formation—tracing, drawing, colouring, making writing patterns (for example ⟨⟨⟨⟨⟨⟨), copying.

Copying is inclined to be controversial. It is sometimes regarded as old-fashioned and boring. This can be true if too much of it is required or if it is undertaken as a kind of drill. It is quite unnecessary to take it to this extreme, but if the child is denied the opportunity for practice he cannot acquire sufficient skill to reach the point when writing is no longer laborious.

Notes

1. At first some children make rows of scribbles (perhaps quite neatly and carefully) which they firmly believe to be 'writing'. They do not yet realise that writing is the transcription of certain conventional letter shapes, and that the hieroglyphics which they devise themselves do not qualify. Time, experience, teaching and practice will lead them to a realisation of what writing really is.

2. Accept mirror writing at this stage. It is extremely common and most children grow out of it.

3. Encourage the child to write from left to right, without making too great an issue of it. A mark at the top left-hand corner of the page, to show him where to begin, helps to establish the habit.

4. Discourage the use of capitals in the wrong places. If children have begun to write at home, it is often the capitals that are taught and some 'unlearning' is then necessary.

5. Writing should be done in books as soon as possible. Sometimes a drawing or a piece of writing may be done on a sheet of paper so that it can be taken home; but if there are too many odd bits of paper they get crumpled and lost and writing becomes undervalued.

Give each child a sugar-paper folder to keep in his locker. His tracings and drawings can be stored in it and after a while the best ones selected and stapled into a book. He can decorate the cover and have his name on it, and he then has something attractive and durable which is really worth taking home.

6. Accept the best that a child can do, but do not give in-

discriminate praise to the scribbles of a child who is capable of something better. There is very great variation in children's ability to master the technical skill at this stage.

NEWS AND DIARIES

'News time', in its traditional form, is unsatisfactory. Children do not have great adventures to report every day, and the content of discussion soon degenerates into the 'I watched the telly' variety in which no one has the smallest interest. However, a time for discussion, for giving children opportunities for self-expression, for helping them to develop language and for providing material for learning to read and write is valuable, and the benefits of the old 'news time' should be retained without its disadvantages. There are one or two things the teacher can do which help to achieve this.

1. Give the children a subject for discussion, in advance. Ask them one day to look particularly for something unusual on their way home or when they come to school the next morning. It is surprising how much children will notice when they have a reason for doing so. 'I saw a cat running up a tree.' 'I saw some men digging a big hole in the road.' 'I saw a wedding car with white ribbons.' 'There was an aeroplane making smoke.' These are ordinary things, but children will talk about them. On another day, ask them to tell you about things they have made in school. The day after that, suggest a theme for tomorrow: the pets that you have, the games you play, the toys you like best, things you like touching. Other possibilities: walk round the school and see what different colours there are, what noises you hear, what shiny things you notice. Shut your eyes and pretend you are standing in the rain. What does it feel like? What do you hear? What would you see?

By giving children a theme or subject there is likely to be more interest and liveliness in discussion and the risk of boredom and of an artificial straining after something to say is much reduced.

2. With very young children, keep the discussion period really short—not more than about ten or fifteen minutes. They are disinclined to listen to what other children are saying and to go on longer than this invites fidgeting and boredom.

3. Make particular efforts to draw out those who are quiet and reserved. Avoid the situation in which the most articulate children monopolise the discussion time.

4. Do not feel obliged to conduct the discussion with the whole class every time, especially if there is a wide age range. Gather together a small group while the others are busy with something else. Quiet or timid children are more likely to respond when not so many are listening.

5. Sometimes, though not necessarily always, choose one item of interest that has been discussed, and write it on a sheet of paper for the class magazine or diary. This must be done very expeditiously and the children must participate as much as possible in assembling the words.

A quick way of doing it is to have a sheet of kitchen paper which you fold to provide guide-lines for your writing. With a large bulldog clip fix it to a convenient flat surface—the back of the standard book corner is excellent for the purpose. Use a fat wax crayon to write the sentence, with the children watching and helping.

Begin with 'the name of today'. Having established that it is Friday, ask a child to find 'Friday' on the days-of-the-week chart. Do the same thing with any other word which may be displayed somewhere in the room. For example the word 'white' is to be used; someone can find it on the colour chart. 'We want "saw" and we used it yesterday'; help a child to find it on yesterday's sheet. The children watch you forming the letters; you talk incidentally about one or two letters as you form them. Your crayon moves from left to right and from top to bottom. You are making many teaching points as you do all this and a great deal of incidental learning is going on. But it must not take long, or the children will switch off.

The completed sheet is then pinned up, and someone may illustrate it later in the day.

The sheet can, if you wish, provide the material for some children to copy, while others have their turn that day for you to write in each child's book at his dictation. Remember that at first some children will not be able to copy from the sheet or from the blackboard. They cannot make the jump from there to their books and remember an outline for long enough to be able to transcribe it. They can copy only from writing that is on their tables, for example a writing card of some kind. In due course they will reach the stage when they can copy from something which is further away.

This kind of reading and writing activity need not take place every day. But it does present you with valuable teaching opportunities, and provided it is conducted fairly briskly, with interesting subject matter, and with the children participating in assembling the writing, there is much to be said for using it as one means of helping them to learn some of the basic reading and writing skills.

FLASH CARDS

It is doubtful whether flash cards, if used merely as a means of giving children practice in rapid word recognition, do very much at this early stage to help them to learn to read. Either a child knows the word or he does not and the same few children answer quickly while the others gain very little from the exercise.

However, it is possible for flash cards to be put to better use than this, and a few minutes with them now and again can help reading along. Those that are available with reading schemes usually contain the words in the early books, but if no scheme is used the teacher can make her own with the common words she wants the children to learn to recognise.

It is useful to have the flash card words duplicated on a chart or on word cards that are pinned up in the room. The teacher then selects five or six words for today's activity. Before holding up the first word, she says that she does not want anyone to say what it is until later; but it is written somewhere else in the room and she wants John to take the flash card and find its 'twin'. She then displays the card and gives it to John who sets off to match it to the duplicate. The teacher, and other children who spot it quickly, can help John with a 'getting warmer' game. Finally the word is matched, John or another child says what it is, something about its shape or appearance is discussed, and John keeps the card. John might well be a child who would never be the first to recognise a word if they were simply held up for recognition, but by this means he has participated in the matching and recognition operation.

When all the cards are finished they are returned to the pack and the children have a game of 'finding the hidden word'. It may be the word 'went'. The teacher first shows this word and helps the children with possible recognition clues. It is then buried a few cards down in the pack and as each word is displayed the children say whether or not it is 'went'. Because they are looking for a specified word they are concentrating much more closely on looking for particular clues, and when the word comes up there is more reinforcement in its recognition. A few minutes' activity when words are carefully observed as part of a game which children enjoy gives flash cards a useful teaching purpose.

Letters on flash cards should be about 3 cm high (excluding ascenders and descenders), and the cards should all be of uniform size in order that an irrelevant clue such as the length of a card plays no part in recognising words.

APPARATUS

Many teachers find it necessary to provide children with material additional to that which can be supplied by the school; apart from this, it is difficult to meet the learning requirements of individual children without recourse to apparatus which is specially prepared to accommodate their needs. For these reasons, some ideas for apparatus appropriate to pre-readers are given below, and though most of these are well known to experienced teachers the suggestions may be helpful to those who have not yet taught children at the pre-reading stage.

Most of it is matching apparatus of one kind or another, since at this stage children need experience of recognising similarities and distinguishing differences. There are three main stages of matching:

(i) Picture to picture.
(ii) Word to word.
(iii) Word to picture.

The first is really a nursery stage, although some children when they reach the reception class may not yet have progressed beyond it. Details of apparatus for this stage are not given here because they are obvious, but certainly such material should be provided for those children who still need it.

The third stage, a picture of a cat, with the word 'cat' on a separate small card which the child has to match to the picture, is more advanced and belongs to the next stage—the 'beginners'. This will therefore be left to the next chapter.

It is the second stage, of word-to-word matching, that in the main applies to the pre-readers. The word may be accompanied by a picture, which gives an added clue to help recognition; or there may be no picture (only nouns, or short phrases containing nouns, can be illustrated), but this material gives children experience of observing similarities and differences in shape and outline—important recognition elements. Examples of both kinds of apparatus are given.

1. A card measuring approximately 25 cm by 30 cm, containing about six small pictures with a word or short phrase written below each. One could be, for example, a picture of a dog; 'dog' might be written below it, or perhaps 'a big dog', in order to familiarise the child with common words which cannot by themselves be illustrated. The identical words or phrases are also written on separate small cards which the child matches to the large one.

Several of these cards will be needed to cover a wide enough range of words.

2. A card 25 cm by 30 cm with one large composite picture in the middle and lines drawn to connect one item in the picture (for example the dog) with the word 'dog' written in the margin; separate small word cards for matching.

3. A 'lotto' game, for four children (Figure 1). Four large cards, each card ruled off with a coloured felt tipped pen into eight sections. Each section contains one word and there is a pack of duplicate matching word cards.

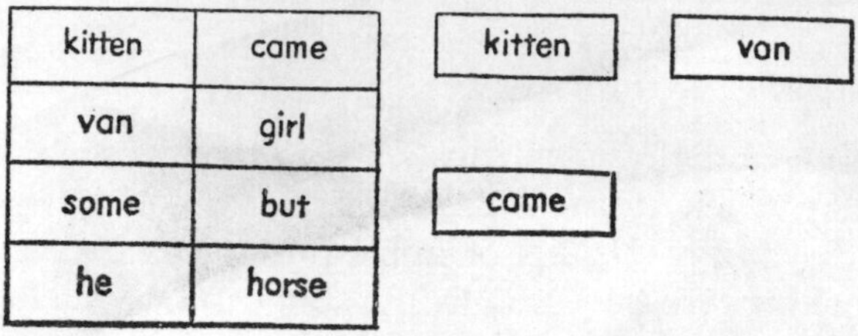

kitten	came
van	girl
some	but
he	horse

kitten		van

came

Figure 1

One of the four children holds up each word from the pack until it is claimed by the child on whose card it appears. The game is finished when all the cards in the pack have been claimed.

4. Dominoes (Figure 2). These may be designed in two ways:

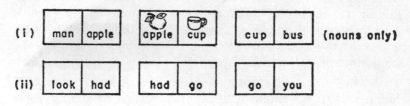

Figure 2

5. Picture/word jigsaws (Figure 3). Strictly speaking, this is a 'beginners' activity; but the jigsaw element helps the pre-reader and with this no harm is done by anticipating the next stage.

Figure 3

6. Manilla strips (Figure 4), folded and stapled to form pockets, with a word written on the *outside* of each pocket; separate word cards to be matched and put in the right pocket.

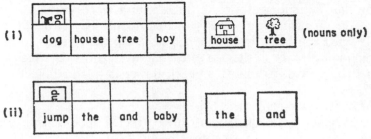

Figure 4

(i) can also be used at the next stage by the beginners, if another set of separate small cards is made showing only the picture and not the word.

7. A variation of 6, to help children to observe the outlines of letters: the letter is written on the pocket and there arc corresponding letters on the small cards.

This may also be used by the beginners if a set of separate picture cards is provided—for example, a picture of a bird to go into the pocket with the initial sound 'b'.

8. A fishing game: small cardboard fish, on each of which a word is written. There are staples in the nose of the fish and the child has a fishing rod with a string tied to a magnet.

For pre-readers, there is a small word chart containing each word, and as the child retrieves a fish he matches it to the corresponding word on the chart.

For beginners, there is a chart containing only pictures and the child matches his fish to the picture. The fish on which the nouns appear should be a different colour from the others, since only these can be matched to pictures.

9. A flower garden (Figure 5): a large piece of sugar paper

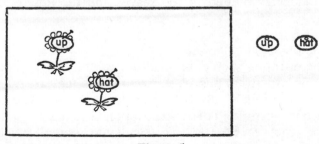

Figure 5

on the wall shows flower outlines with a word written in the centre of each. The small word card fills the centre of the flower. Each has a hole punched in it. On the chart there is a pin or small tack at the top of each flower centre, on which the matching cards are hung as each flower is 'planted'.

Miscellaneous material

1. *Tracing cards.* The picture to be traced should have very simple outlines, with a caption below. Mount the pictures on cards and provide a supply of tracing paper cut to size. If children have difficulty in holding the paper in place, fix it on the card with a paper clip.

2. *Writing cards:* about 25 cm by 30 cm, with a picture at the top and some writing below for the children to copy. The writing should be large and clear. There can also be writing on the back of the card for those whose skill is increasing and who can accomplish more.

3. *Odd minute cards.* These suggest short practical tasks which are useful for 'early finishers': draw two fish, make a train with bricks, trace a picture, draw a picture of yourself, do some weighing, find three red beads and draw them, read a book. The teacher must read the card for the child; but the card gives him a purpose and something particular to do in the odd minutes when there is hardly time for him to apply himself to anything more protracted.

4. *Name cards.* Make one for each child. His name should be written in large letters. Encourage him to learn to trace or copy it, and later to write it himself.

5. *Writing patterns.* Have some cards with writing patterns on them for a child to trace or copy. These are very helpful in introducing children to the shapes and the flow of handwriting.

Some notes about apparatus

1. All apparatus should be made to a really high standard. Never use capitals at this stage except where they are essential; unnecessary capitals only complicate word outlines. Use colour as much as possible. Illustration is often required at this stage. For the teacher whose artistic talents are limited, much can be achieved with simple diagrammatic outlines and attractive

colour presentation. Alternatively pictures can be cut from magazines, or they can be bought in packs from educational suppliers.

2. Small matching cards are apt to stray. A symbol on the back of all those that belong together helps to identify the pieces and children can then sort them out. Train them to do this and to keep the material in order. It is helpful to punch a hole in each card and string together with a treasury tag all those that are part of one piece of apparatus. Even very young children can learn to thread and unthread these quite easily.

3. When children have matched their apparatus, they should trace or copy at least some of the words they have matched. This 'kinaesthetic learning' is a valuable addition to learning by sight and sound.

4. When children are using matching apparatus, it is essential that the teacher should make available a few minutes for each child, to help him 'read' the words he has matched, to talk about their shape, appearance, etc. and to help him with the processes of word recognition. Without this teaching, much if not most of the value of the activity is lost.

CHARTS

Certain wall charts are especially helpful at this stage, and some of them will continue to be useful at later stages.

1. Charts of familiar nursery rhymes: from time to time the children can 'read' these while singing them in unison, and as the teacher points along the line while the children sing the words they learn about the direction of written English. Odd words or phrases can occasionally be isolated and conversationally discussed. Familiar poems can be similarily treated.

2. A chart of the days of the week: writing them in different colours helps identification. The 'name of today' can be found each morning, and the name of tomorrow or yesterday. The words can also be found for use with news sheets etc.

3. A colour chart, the colour being shown beside each word.

4. A weather chart: separate cards describe the weather, and the children learn to identify them by finding the word that applies each day.

Charts should not be put on the wall and left there without frequent reference being made to them. In spare minutes, do some 'wall reading', 'What are the words on this chart?' 'Susan, show me where to find the word "sunny".' In this way, children will learn to look for words that are around them, and later when they begin doing their own writing they can find some of the words for themselves.

When a chart no longer serves a useful purpose, remove it and replace it with a new one. Do not let charts become an unnoticed part of the classroom scenery. If this happens, they cease to have much value.

ORGANISATION AND PLANNING

It is not easy to organise a class of very young children. If the class is family-grouped and only a few are at the beginning of their school lives, the organisational problems are in some ways less acute. But if all or most of the children are at the 'reception' stage, the teacher's organisation must be structured in such a way that it is very clearly recognisable to them. As far as reading and writing are concerned, there are several considerations which must be taken into account.

1. Give the children plenty of help and guidance with regard to what there is for them to do. Begin by directing them to clearly defined tasks. This is probably most easily done in groups: this group is to begin drawing a picture of whatever the children want to write about, while the teacher goes round and writes the words at each child's dictation; at the same time that group has tracing cards, a third group has something else (probably a mathematics activity). The important thing is that the teacher should make sure the children *know exactly what they are supposed to be doing.* At a later stage the group pattern will become much more individual and the children will be able to make more of their own decisions without feeling bewildered and consequently lacking in direction and purpose.

2. If one group has an activity which is likely to need a good deal of help, plan activities for the others which they can more easily manage with less attention.

3. Because the span of concentration of young children is short, allow for frequent change of activity.

4. Let all the class come together every now and again for a few minutes of songs, movement poems, rhymes and jingles, or a story. This helps to avoid the disintegration which happens only too easily with a large class of small children who are not yet able to do very much about organising themselves.

5. List all the reading and writing activities appropriate to this level of development, and select from your list certain activities for each group each day. Do not forget to include in your plans opportunities for any direct teaching which you think a group needs. Remember, too, that 'activities' in this sense include not only group and individual 'tasks', but also the experiences which you know to be necessary for linguistic development and for the children's intellectual and emotional satisfaction. Keep sufficiently detailed records to ensure that all the children have access, in turn, to the activities which you regard as necessary to their progress.

Chapter 11

The Beginners in the Classroom

THE CHILDREN

Generally speaking, children reach this stage of reading comparatively quickly—perhaps within a few weeks of starting school, though of course there are exceptions. In terms of personal development, therefore, they have not changed a very great deal and such change as has taken place is mainly in emphasis rather than in the emergence of any really different characteristics. The change of emphasis manifests itself in various ways:

1. They are still highly individualistic, though they are beginning to take a bit more notice of what other children are doing and they are a little more inclined to make a joint effort in pairs or in small groups. Any topic work must still take account of this.

2. Except in a very few cases, they are now quite settled in school. Their initial bewilderment with a way of life that is so different from home has disappeared and they are aware that they are beginning to learn how to read and write. Many of them are becoming very enthusiastic about it.

3. Individual interests and skills are emerging quite markedly. This affects the teacher's planning and the ways in which she tries to motivate individual children to learn. The gap between the most and the least advanced is widening.

4. Likes and dislikes are noticeable. Groupings and friendships are beginning to show, though they may be of only very short duration.

5. The children can concentrate on one task for a little longer —perhaps for about twenty minutes (though this is a rather arbitrary kind of figure, and it will vary with the nature of the task).

6. They can work a little more on their own, if they are trained to do so. They can find some of their own materials and put them away after use—again, if they are trained to do so. This training is now very necessary, because these children are quite capable of profiting by it.

7. If they are at ease in school they will talk and discuss more freely, with each other and with the teacher. There are still immense differences in experience and linguistic ability—in some ways the differences are greater. Discussion, both planned and incidental, is still vital.

8. The children should still approach topic work in much the same way as they did at the pre-reading stage and the subjects in which they are likely to be interested are similar. Some degree of development in their skills and their reactions will, however, be apparent.

9. They still need very clear instructions about what to do, though some can now organise their efforts over a longer time span. The teacher can, for example, tell some of the more capable and confident children of two things she would like them to do, in the order of their choice, and they can move on to the second when they have finished the first without intermediate reference to her.

10. There is no difference in the children's dependence on a good pupil/teacher relationship. Indeed, this condition remains throughout the First School.

OBJECTIVES AND IDEAS FOR READING

1. The 'beginners' are now at the point when reading is beginning to mean something to them. They know what 'reading' is —that is, they know which written patterns are words and which are not, that reading involves 'decoding' the written patterns, that only certain particular marks represent a word, that the direction of our written language is from left to right and from top to bottom.

2. With regard to some of the materials which the teacher provides, this is a difficult stage. The children can recognise similarities and differences in outlines and they can match words and phrases instantly; but they cannot yet read many of

the words they have matched. Some ideas for apparatus which may help with this problem are given later.

3. They know some words by sight, but usually only when they meet them in an expected context. They may, for example, recognise 'little' on a flash card or familiar word chart but not when they see it in a book from the book corner.

4. If a reading scheme is used, the children at this stage are ready for the introductory book. As a very rough and ready guide this is often taken to be when about ten sight words from the book are known. If no scheme is used, reading should begin from a very simple book selected by the teacher.

5. Once some children in the class have reading books there is a great demand for them from all the others. The time will fairly quickly come when all but a few have them and here the teacher must use her judgement. It is often advisable to let all the remaining children have a book even though they may not really be ready for it; otherwise they are afflicted with a sense of failure, and this is more damaging than having a book too soon. However, the teacher avoids pressing these children to read the book while giving them every encouragement to try if they want to do so.

6. In planned discussion periods, the children at this stage still have difficulty in thinking of things to talk about. So the teacher continues to give them ideas and themes for discussion along much the same lines as with the pre-readers. However, such discussion will now be a little more sophisticated, a little more articulate and rather more spontaneous—but not *much* more than at the pre-reading stage.

7. Reading is now beginning in connection with other activities, for example in mathematics; but the common words and phrases which are being used—'count', 'how many', 'buy', 'balance', etc. should be deliberately taught, with flash cards, word charts, matching games and so on.

8. The most significant difference from the pre-reading stage is that the beginners understand what reading is about. They cannot yet do it, but they are ready to begin and they are *ready to be taught*.

OBJECTIVES AND IDEAS FOR WRITING

As far as writing is concerned, the children's needs and the teacher's techniques are very little different in kind as compared with the earlier stage, but there is a noticeable difference in emphasis and quality. Much that was said in the previous chapter therefore still applies, but with some modification.

1. Some children can now control a pencil quite skilfully. Most can copy, including from the blackboard or a news sheet. As was discussed in an earlier chapter, there are bound to be some quite advanced children who are still experiencing very real difficulty with the technical skill and they need time, practice, patience and encouragement. But only the very backward children will, when they have been in school a term or so, still be making rows of unidentifiable marks in the belief that they are 'writing'.

2. The children will not yet be able to compose and write an original sentence, though some may be on the verge of doing so. The teacher will still be acting as 'secretary' and writing for them at their dictation. They are, however, more competent at telling the teacher what to write, in a form suitable for writing. They have more ideas of what to write about, and because their technical skill has improved they can write more and their sentences are longer. This becomes very demanding on the teacher's time and she has to organise it carefully so that all groups in turn have a share of her secretarial services.

3. There is still value in the writing follow-up of discussion, on the 'news sheet' principle. But again, it flows more freely, words are found more easily, more may be written. This activity, however, will gradually diminish and will disappear by the time the children reach the stage discussed in the next chapter.

4. At this stage there is much to commend in the *Breakthrough to Literacy*[1] principle of children assembling pre-written words to make sentences of their own choosing. It is very helpful in

[1] Mackay *et al.*

bridging the gap until they can perform the whole operation of composing and writing a sentence 'from scratch'.

FLASH CARDS

These may still be used in much the same way as in the pre-reading stage, but the operation can be faster and more words can be dealt with. The use of flash cards in this form will diminish and disappear before the next stage is reached.

APPARATUS

This is probably the most difficult stage for which to design effective apparatus. The children are past the word-to-word matching stage and yet they cannot read any but the very few words which by now they know by sight. Card apparatus now falls broadly into four categories, but it is difficult to find a great deal of variation in material that is really appropriate to this stage. The four categories are:

  (i) Word to picture matching (for examples, see Chapter 10, apparatus item 5, and the variations of items 6 and 8; also items 1 and 2 below).

 (ii) A rather more sophisticated form of word-to-word and letter-to-letter matching (items 3, 4, 5 and 6 below).

(iii) The first simple phonic apparatus, including some which draws the child's attention to symbols as parts of words (the variation of item 7 in Chapter 10, and items 7 and 8 below).

(iv) Very simple straightforward reading (items 9 and 10 below).

Examples of apparatus appropriate to this stage are:
1. A card 25 cm by 30 cm containing about six small pictures representing nouns and short phrases that include nouns, drawn from a fairly carefully controlled vocabulary of words which the children meet frequently. (If a reading scheme is used most of the words will be taken from the introductory book); separate small cards containing the words to be matched to the pictures.

2. Picture/word dominoes:

Do not make the mistake of having a word and a picture on the same card, or confusion will result. Have two pictures or two words on each card.

3. Strips containing sentences from the introductory reading book; a box of all the words in the book. The child takes a strip, matches the words, finds the sentence in the book, reads it to the teacher and then copies it to reinforce the learning.

4. A pack of cards each with a word or phrase which is illustrated; a box of letters. The child selects the letters to match the word. The purpose of the illustration is to help the child begin making the association between the appearance of some of the letters and their sounds—perhaps the initial letter and sound of each word to begin with.

Instead of a pack of cards, the large cards in item 1 may be used for this purpose. This item could also belong to category (iii).

5. The box of letters from item 4, which the child matches to the words of his own 'news' sentence.

6. An introductory reading book or other inexpensive familiar 'first book', which is cut up, with each page mounted on manilla, to be used in one of the following ways:

(a) Cut off the writing and mount each phrase or sentence strip on separate pieces of manilla. From the illustration, the child finds the page in a duplicate book, then finds the correct sentence strips, matches them to his picture and copies the words for reinforcement.

(b) As in (a), but cut the writing into separate words instead of sentence strips.

(c) Cut a word or two out of the writing on a page and replace them with dashes. For example the sentence 'The kitten plays with a ball' might read 'The - - - - - - plays with a - - - -'. The child finds the missing words in the duplicate book, assembles them from the box of letters and then copies the sentence.

7. A card containing three of four phrases in which one letter is frequently repeated, for example:

> Cover every 'a'
> Pat ate an apple.
> I saw a cat.
> A black cat.
> Mary has a hat.

Have a box containing small blank cards for covering the 'a's . The child, with the teacher's help, reads the phrases, then copies and illustrates one.

This piece of apparatus is on the 'put a ring round' principle but avoids the necessity of defacing the card, so it may be used again by other children.

8. 'Find all the words in the word box which begin with "p" '; from a list of words 'Copy all the words which begin with "p" ' or 'Copy these words, and put a ring round all those with "sh" in them.' With some of these, the written instruction is rather long and the child will not be able to read it. The design of the card can help to overcome this problem. For example, the 'Copy all the words which begin with "p" ' cards can all be made with a blue border and the letter—in this example 'p'—written in red. The child learns what to do with the cards designed in this particular way, and thus there is no need for the written instruction to be interpreted for him every time. Indeed, the full written instruction is not really necessary unless the teacher wants to have it.

9. A picture, with two simple sentences below it, only one of which describes the picture, for example a picture of a girl, and the sentences

'This is Mary', 'This is John'.

The child selects and copies the correct sentence.

10. Have a box of words, taken from the introductory or other familiar first book. The nouns (naming words) are on orange card, the verbs (doing words) on green and all others on blue. The child tries to assemble phrases and sentences before reading and copying them. This is fairly difficult at this stage, but it can be used by children who are almost at the stage of being

'advanced readers'. The fact that the words are taken from a very familiar book makes it easier and the exercise really helps children to understand the principle of assembling words into sentences.

CHARTS

In addition to the charts used at the pre-reading stage, a set of 'alphabet' charts can now begin coming into use. For each letter there should be a clear, single picture illustrating a word which begins with the *sound* of the letter (not its alphabetic name). Care must be taken with some of the pictures. For example, a picture of an owl will not do for 'o', because the word 'owl' does not begin with the short vowel sound, whereas the word 'orange' does. A composite picture of a basket of oranges on a table will not do either. because it will not be clear whether the letter is to be associated with the initial sound of 'oranges' or 'basket' or 'table'. Pictures which could be described by more than one noun should also be avoided; for example, a picture of a mat might be either 'mat' or 'rug'. There are two letters which can have either a hard or soft sound, 'c' and 'g'. Although the picture can illustrate only one of the sounds, the children's attention should be drawn from the start to the fact that there are two alternatives.

The *Ladybird* alphabet book[2] contains excellent pictures for these charts. They are clear and well produced, and on the whole they represent the sounds accurately. If only the lower case letters are shown beside each picture, they should be printed on a line to indicate ascenders and descenders, for example a b g Otherwise children tend to write g. Alternatively, the upper and lower case letters can be shown side by side, for example P p

At this stage these charts should not be introduced to children formally, or for the purpose of 'learning the alphabet'. One way of beginning is to make use of a word which has arisen in discussion. There might have been, let us say, some discussion about a tree. Quite informally the teacher would ask the children to say the word 'tree' and try and think of the first 'noise' they make when they say it. This is established,

[2] Published by Wills & Hepworth.

and 'tree' written on the blackboard with the initial letter emphasised. The children are then invited to try and think of some more words which begin with the same noise. There will be several suggestions; some will be right and others will not. Each word beginning with 't' is written up, with the first letter stressed, and the incorrect suggestions tactfully overlooked because these children are at a very early stage of phonic training.

When a few words beginning with 't' have been found, the 't' chart is produced, the picture and its initial sound discussed, the outline of the symbol (perhaps upper as well as lower case) examined and any particular characteristics in the shape of the outline noted. The chart is then pinned on the wall and, as with all other charts, reference is made to it from time to time. In a few weeks, several of the alphabet charts will have been assembled, in the order in which they will eventually be placed when the alphabet is complete.

We should recognise that the purpose of using alphabet charts at this stage is simply to familiarise children with the letters and to begin, very informally, making some of the associations between sound and symbol. These charts do not introduce the child to all the symbol/sound relationships he will ultimately need. They are concerned only with single letters and they do not take account of all the exceptions, such as the 'v' sound in 'of'. Nevertheless, they do perform some useful functions; they help children to become familiar with the appearance of letters; they introduce the *principle* of symbol/ sound association; and they provide a visual *aide-mémoire* for letter formation and for the simple phonic apparatus which by now is making an appearance. Provided the charts are not used at this stage to support abstract word building or tiresome phonic drill they can be of practical help to the children who are just beginning to read.

ORGANISATION AND PLANNING

There is little at this stage that is very different from that which is needed for pre-readers. The children are a little more capable, they will continue at one task for a bit longer than before, their powers of organising themselves from one activity to another have advanced slightly, and though the teacher's instructions to them must still be clear and unambiguous she can assume a relatively more sophisticated reaction in the way in which the children will put them into effect. It has already been suggested, for example, that the teacher can now ask them to undertake two areas of activity and leave it to them to accomplish both with only minimal organisational guidance from her; and that in the matter of using materials the children can act more independently. In other words, the teacher's organisation and planning are substantially the same as they were for the pre-readers, but she can allow for the variation in detail and emphasis which the children's more advanced level of development now permits.

The one organisational area for which she must now make additional provision is that which concerns her arrangements for hearing reading. She has, in effect, been 'hearing reading' since the beginning. The minute or two she has spent with each child helping him to begin identifying some of the words on his matching apparatus, the writing she has done at his dictation of words which they have then 'read' together, the time spent on finding and identifying words for the 'news sheet'—in all these aspects of her teaching she has, in fact, been hearing reading. However, many of these activities are still continuing during this present stage and the teacher must, in addition, hear the children read to her from the first books to which they now proudly feel themselves to have been promoted. It is important that this aspect of organisation and planning is not neglected and for this reason it has been given detailed attention in Chapter 9.

Chapter 12

The Advancing Readers in the Classroom

THE CHILDREN

By the time children have emerged from the 'beginners' stage to that of the 'advancing readers' they have taken a considerable step forward in terms of their personal development. This is not, of course, a sudden transformation. As in all stages of development the movement from one to the next is a process of merging rather than of immediate change. But in so far as any level of development is characterised by certain personal and intellectual features, there is evident in the advancing readers a notable degree of progress since the time when they were just moving towards an understanding of the printed word. This is distinguishable in a number of ways.

1. Though individualistic behaviour is still evident (this remains a characteristic throughout the First School years) the children are now appreciably more interested in contributing to some kind of group or even class activity.

2. Their horizons are widening and projects or topics need not be so directly connected with their personal affairs.

3. They can apply themselves, for longer periods, with more persistence and greater interest. Obviously there is variation, but most of these children can remain on one task for about half an hour without too much effort.

4. Provided they are trained to do so, they can exercise a greater degree of independence and initiative. The teacher's organisation must still provide a sound and recognisable structure for learning, as it must throughout the First School, but within this framework the children can accept more responsibility for organising themselves than they could before.

Instructions, though obviously they should be clear, need not be broken down into such small packets since the children will much less easily misunderstand or forget what they are asked to do.[1]

5. The children are markedly more skilful, both physically and intellectually. They will recognise superior and inferior skills among themselves and they will help one another.

6. Leaders have emerged. So have the less laudable characteristics, but the teacher can depend upon more direct co-operation among the children in dealing with the troublesome members of the class. This does not imply the encouragement of self-righteous behaviour, but simply that the opinion and influence of peers are beginning to count.

7. The problem of variation in experience and linguistic skill has not been solved—it really never is. While the teacher has done much to try to compensate for deprivation in these areas, the children whose environmental influences are more favourable continue to benefit from them and their less favoured friends do not often catch up unless they are exceptionally able.

8. Because the children at this level of development have come such a long way it is easy to overestimate what can be expected of them. They are so much more skilful that one can forget the close limits of their skill. Their self-confidence, though often apparently secure, is still very precarious and failure over a task that is too difficult can really upset them. Even though they are advancing, many of them are still very young; and this will not infrequently be evident in their reactions in the classroom.

9. The range of ability and achievement between the most and the least advanced is even more noticeable. Both group and individual teaching are essential and much of the approach appropriate to the earlier stages of reading and writing must continue in parallel to that now needed by the advancing readers.

---

[1] The organisation and planning of reading and writing are now absorbed into general organisation, and they will not be given a separate section as in the last two chapters. This is because, by this stage, there are not the specific *organisational* points which can be identified separately from those which apply in all areas of learning.

READING: OBJECTIVES AND POSSIBILITIES

1. The stage of the 'advancing readers' encompasses the child's progress from the time when he really begins to read to the time when he can read pretty fluently. This may be quite a long period, since the advance is considerable. Perhaps this chapter should be divided into more than one stage; but since so much of the activity during these months is basically of a related character, and the changes are those which bring variety, the extension of experience and interest, the introduction of progressively complex reading material and the development of a skill which has emerged and is advancing, it seems preferable not to attempt a somewhat artificial exercise in further subdivision. Certainly there will be graduated steps during this stage and the teacher will naturally pursue a progressive and developmental course. It is for clarity of presentation rather than for the rigid delineation of classroom practice that this extensive reading stage is treated as one.

2. At the beginning of it, the children have made a start with the reading scheme or whatever early reading books are used, and some of them will progress from this point quite quickly. They will accumulate a respectable vocabulary of sight words, but although they will, increasingly, recognise them in unfamiliar contexts this 'transfer' of recognition takes some time to become secure. By the time these children reach the end of the stage they should no longer experience this difficulty.

3. They are familiar at the outset with the majority of letter outlines and during this stage most of the sound/symbol relationships will become well established. Word building, first of regular two and three letter words and later of more complex combinations, will be possible—and, indeed, very necessary—as reading skill develops.

4. The opportunity to express themselves in words and to talk about their interests is as important to the children whose reading is advancing as it was when they were at an earlier level of development. However, it will no longer take the form of an organised period of time devoted to the discussion of matters of immediate personal concern. It will now arise, some-

times almost exclusively, from topics and projects. These are therefore treated more fully later in the chapter.

5. The children will now really begin to appreciate the purpose of reading. It will not be long before they can pick up a simple book in the book corner and find that they can read at least some of it. This will happen on a very limited scale at first, but as the children progress through this stage many of them will experience the pleasure and recognise the value of being able to read the books that are made available for them. They are not likely to read very much for information yet, but some may begin doing so towards the end of this stage.

6. They will now be meeting more material which requires reading in the various areas of their daily activity. At the beginning of this stage, such material must be very simple; it must use only a small vocabulary, with frequent repetition. For example, a measuring card may say: 'Measure the table. How many spans long is it? How many spans wide?' Other cards may ask for similar measurements of various things in the room.

This wording is too complex. There are too many words and sentences and too many different concepts to be absorbed from the written language. The reading requirement is altogether too extensive for the mathematical exercise. It would be better to put an identical heading on every card and reduce the remaining instruction to a minimum, for example:

```
How many spans wide?
  1. table
  2. blackboard
```

Once the children can decode the single instruction at the beginning the rest is fairly easy, especially if the things in the room are labelled.

As they move through this stage the problem diminishes. They should be given every opportunity to read all this other material, but it is important to design it so that the reading is within their capacity or they may become disheartened. They should be encouraged, too, to read books other than those in the reading scheme and to tell the teacher about them whenever time can be found. This, again, extends in scope as reading ability during this stage develops.

7. The realisation that the time has arrived when they are certainly learning to read will be a strong motivation. This will make some children very enthusiastic and the teacher must make use of this enthusiasm to help them develop their reading skill. It is now particularly true that nothing succeeds like success, and there can be quite a rapid 'snowball' effect once children see that their efforts are rewarded with results.

WRITING: OBJECTIVES AND POSSIBILITIES

Personal writing
It is at about this time that children can make the major advance of being able to dispense with the teacher's secretarial services and write a sentence for themselves. This, however, usually needs some very careful and deliberate teaching because it demands a great deal more of the child than the 'dictation' which by now he can do quite easily.

The foundation that was laid earlier has brought him to the point when he

   (i) can decide what he will write about;
  (ii) realises that he must translate his thoughts into a form suitable for writing; and
 (iii) can think of the actual words that are to be written.

He can do these things, but only just; and when he is asked to do them by himself, without the teacher undertaking part of the task, he will not find it easy, even though he has apparently been doing it quite efficiently, with the teacher, for some time.

There is therefore, for most children, an initial stage in this process of writing an original sentence when there is again a need for much the same kind of help as the teacher gave when dictating first began; and when one considers the question, this is not really very surprising. It is one thing to have the teacher beside you, ready with a suggestion or a word of help and, as a joint effort, to do something which was once difficult but has now become comfortably familiar. It is altogether another thing to find yourself depending to a great extent upon your own intellectual resources to do the same thing more or less unaided. It is a bigger step than we sometimes realise, but the foundation that has already been laid ensures that, with the right help, the step is not too big for the child to take. So he will again need

(i) a little help in deciding what to write about—not as much as before, but help which is more in the nature of a reminder and a reassurance; and

(ii) the opportunity to think, before writing anything, of the *exact* words that are to be written. It is this particular requirement which again seems to confuse the child when his 'secretary' is not with him.

The teacher should therefore ask the child to tell her the actual words he proposes to write, for example, 'We did a play about dragons.' She then asks him to repeat the first word of that sentence. She may well be surprised at the effort that is needed before the child realises that the first word to be written is 'we'. However, he then writes it. It may take much the same procedure to establish that the next word is 'did'. The child will, of course, have forgotten the rest of the sentence long before he gets to the end of it and he will need help in recalling it.

It is no exaggeration to say that many children need quite as much help as this before they fully understand the technique of writing an original sentence. It is because of this that they are often thought to be not yet able to write anything themselves and therefore to have to continue with copying. However, it is worth giving them the kind of help that has been suggested as soon as they can dictate really efficiently, because one ought not to delay longer than is necessary the development of the skill of original composition. With some children 'the penny will drop' quite quickly and the production of the first sentence will follow rapidly. With others it will take longer and the teacher will need to continue with this detailed assistance until the child can manage confidently without it.

It could be argued that if a child needs so much help in producing his first original sentence, he is not yet ready to write it and it should therefore not be asked of him. This argument, however, ignores the possible interpretations of the word 'ready'. If we must wait until he is ready to write it without being taught how to do so, then indeed he will not be ready for a long time yet. But readiness to be taught and readiness to acquire a skill without being taught represent two very different educational objectives.

Once the child has acquired the skill of writing his first single sentence, the amount of his personal writing will gradually increase. It will increase, that is, in quantity but not, for some time, in quality. We should let him reach the stage when he can fairly easily and fluently express his thoughts in writing before we ask him to be self-critical about the quality of what he writes.

When he begins to produce a greater quantity of writing, he will join every sentence with 'and' or 'and then'. The teacher must judge with the individual child the time at which it is appropriate to suggest that when he has finished writing one bit, he should put a little dot to show that he has finished and then start a new sentence (with a capital letter as they do in books). It is probably better not to ask much more than this until the child is writing with ease, so a discussion of further improvement in quality will be left until the next chapter. The child who can now express himself comfortably in a few short sentences, simple though they may be, has already come a long way in learning how to write his language.

Once original writing begins the teacher meets, inevitably, the problem of the word queue. This must be tackled at once, because every child who is at this stage will come to her for every word. Two things are therefore essential.

(i) Words must be made available in the room for the child to copy without reference to the teacher.

(ii) The building of simple phonically regular words must be established as a habit.

Making words available

The teacher will very quickly isolate the common everyday words which every child seems to want. The list of 'key words' given in Appendix C may also help her. She will find, for example, that many children still want to write about their families; so she needs a 'family' chart, i.e. pictures of people who might be *Mummy, Daddy, baby, brother, sister*, etc. with the word beside the picture. She will also find that some of the notices around the room can supply a number of much needed words. A notice by the book corner saying 'Come and read a book' includes two of the most commonly needed words, *come* and *and*. 'We have a hamster' supplies *we* and *have*; 'This is the nature table' gives the children *this*, *is* and *the*.

Having worded such notices carefully so that they include some of these common words, the teacher will find it helpful to make a chart (possibly one or two more later on) with other words which are much in demand, such as *was*, *my*, *saw*, *said*, *with*. At this stage, however, it is not very helpful to have charts which are simply lists of words. The children still need clues to help with identification. The use of colour offers one possibility. 'Said' is the word written in blue, 'saw' is the red one, and so on. Another way is to use simple outline shapes, for example:

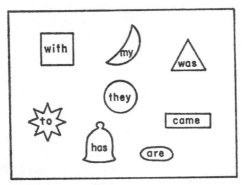

A useful expedient is to make large books to hang up, each of which contains pictures and words connected with a likely area of interest for which words may be required. There may be a 'house' book, for instance, in which there are named pictures of rooms, furniture, domestic activities, etc. Other books may concern clothes, toys, animals, games—anything on which children at this stage tend to draw heavily in describing their activities and interests.

One cannot have a great proliferation of word charts, or there will be too many words for the children to remember; but one or two will be very helpful and when they become really familiar others can be added. Once the children are trained to use them, these charts will do much to reduce the length of the word queue. A minute or two frequently spent on 'wall reading' is very necessary, to remind the children where the words are and to make them really familiar with 'the word that's in the square'. 'Find the word in the room' games also help to achieve this; and of course it is most important that the teacher should insist upon the children using the charts. They will still ask her for some of these words, either because they have forgotten that the word is on a chart or because they cannot be bothered to look for it. Patience and insistence on the teacher's part will eventually overcome this.[2]

Apart from the fact that word charts do reduce the queue they also fulfil a valuable function in helping the child to learn the common words more quickly and with greater reinforcement. If he has to make the effort to identify the word for himself and then copy it in his book, more learning will take place than if he simply gets the teacher to write it in his word book and, having copied it, forgets all about it. Copying comes before remembering; even in adult life we 'copy' from a dictionary a word of which we are unsure. But copying which has required a personal effort of identification will help the memorising process.

The child will still need his word book, because clearly every word he is likely to want cannot appear on a chart. He should try to open the book at the correct alphabetical page before presenting it to the teacher, though he will need help with this until he reaches the stage when his phonic training enables him to do it on his own. Even then he will run into problems, like opening the book at page 's' for 'smornin'—'smornin when I came to school. . . .'

Phonic word building

Some of the foundations for word building were laid in the earlier stage, but this should now be approached more systematically. Many of the short common words that children want are phonically regular, for instance *at, in, if, had, went*. However, even though these children are now fairly familiar with many of the symbols and their sounds the teacher must at this stage ensure that phonic skills are developed and firmly consolidated.

[2] For some more ideas about word charts and their use, see Taylor, *Organising and Integrating the Infant Day*, pp. 32–3.

She will find that with many children it is necessary to show them how to fuse sounds so that they come together to make a word. She may start by sounding, with the children, the 'noises' of the separate letters *u, p*; the 'noises' are then said faster and faster until they have run together and the word is made. Next they may try *c, u, p*, and they make another word. It will not take long before the children recognise the principle of what they are doing and they can then understand how to fuse sounds to make words themselves. (The common letter groups which produce a single sound, such as *sh, th*, etc., should also be understood at this stage.)

The connection must now be made between fusing sounds and writing the symbols which represent them. Games can be devised to make this more interesting. Two children can hold up papers on which are written *a* and *n*; the others direct them so that they stand side by side in the correct order to make the word *an*. A third child has a *d* and must be directed so as to make *and*; another has an *l* and the word becomes *land*. It is changed to *band, sand, hand, hands*. In this way the children learn how to unite symbols to form words, just as they learned how to synthesise sounds.[3]

That phonic training of this kind must now be undertaken is inescapable. It need not, however, be a dreary drill. Any teacher will be able to think of simple games which are enjoyable but which at the same time develop phonic skills; and during this stage the children can be given many of the games in the Stott *Programmed Reading Kit*,[4] which they can play by themselves and which provide similar opportunities. Teacher-made apparatus can also be devised to give them additional experience.

The technical skill of writing

In the earlier stages all that was required of the children was that they should, with encouragement, example and practice, learn to form letters and copy words to the best of their ability and as legibly as their skill would allow. By now, the majority of them will be doing this reasonably effortlessly and during

[3] For guidance on the order in which it may be advantageous to introduce the sounds of letters and letter combinations, see Appendix D.
[4] D. H. Stott, op. cit.

this stage their technical skill can be advanced. There are a few guide-lines which may be helpful here:

1. Spaces between words and lines must now be required as a habit. (For any children who are in doubt, the space of one finger between words and two fingers between lines gives them a helpful guide.)

2. Reject scribbly writing, but accept the best he can do from the child who still has genuine difficulty.

3. To begin with, plain paper is preferable, though the children will probably move to lined paper before they reach the end of this stage.

4. Still accept mirror writing, though it should now decrease rapidly. Casually point out the difference without giving the impression that mirror writing is reprehensible.

5. Continue to draw attention to the correct formation of letters in any writing that the children see you doing.

6. Teach the full stop, and the use of capitals for proper names and at the beginning of a sentence. The question mark may be introduced incidentally; it will appear on apparatus on which questions are asked so it should be explained.

7. Do not correct every word that is wrongly written. Correct only the mistakes which the child *at his level of development* should not have made. At the beginning of this stage virtually no mistakes will come into this category; but as the child advances the question of correction will begin to arise. Remember that it is always better to correct too little than to correct too much. Never make the child rewrite the word correctly. Tell him of the mistake and encourage him to try to put it right the next time.

By the end of this stage many children are writing fairly fluently, though they are still using a simple vocabulary and sentence structure. They have, however, made a very considerable advance as compared with their level of achievement when they began to write their first original sentence, and they are ready to move towards the more sophisticated written language which fluency in the basic skill now makes possible.

TOPICS AND PROJECTS

Very early in this stage topics and projects begin to provide one of the main sources of ideas for discussion and for the development of the language skills which continue to be an essential element of learning to read and write. They do not, of course, displace the incidental conversational contact between teacher and child or among groups of children; nor does the reporting of day-to-day events and experiences cease, either at this or at any other stage. These conversational occasions continue for personal, social, intellectual and emotional reasons. But the kind of discussion that is expressly orientated towards the growth of interests and the development of language is now likely to be very much concerned with group or class activities connected with an organised centre of interest.

In the early part of this period such activity will not be as coherent as it will be later on. It does, however, quite soon take place on a more advanced scale than at the earlier stages. It involves more children and it lasts longer. It gradually becomes more diverse and it ranges over a greater variety of interest and activity as the children progress. The teacher can, increasingly, draw upon ideas which are outside the children's immediate experience as they develop the capacity to comprehend something about people and places which they do not know.

However, the children cannot yet search out their own information from books. Although their reading skill is advancing they are not able to extract and summarise information from written sources unless this is very simply and directly presented. The teacher will find it extremely beneficial, for example, to mount pictures concerned with the topic on cards and write an explanatory phrase or sentence beneath each picture. This might range from a very simple statement in the early part of this period, for example 'a log cabin', to more detailed information about log cabins and where they are found when the children's reading skill has increased. But one cannot expect the child, even towards the end of this stage, to 'find out about log cabins' from a book. A requirement that he should do so invariably results in passages being copied word for word, which benefits neither the child nor the project. Information must therefore be made available to the children in a more concise and selective form.

Although they can now engage in topics which are outside their personal experience, they do need a great deal of visual material to give interest and meaning to such subjects. Pictures, coloured slides, film strips and objects of interest concerned with the topic are essential. Provided, however, that the teacher will prepare the ground by making this kind of material available, topics on a wide variety of subjects can be made interesting and realistic and can supply the means by which experience is extended and language, both spoken and written, enriched. Even such subjects as other lands and peoples, other ages of history and occupations and ways of life which the children do not know (fishing, lumberjacking, space travel, exploration) can have meaning and reality, as long as they are presented in a form which recognises the children's limitations and with material appropriate to their level of understanding.

APPARATUS

It is now much easier to provide children with materials other than those which the teacher makes herself for the development of their reading and writing skills. For this reason, and because it is not so hard to devise apparatus as reading ability increases, only a selection of ideas, varied in difficulty, is given for this stage:

1. Jumbled letter cards, with pictures for clues, for example a picture of a hat, with the letters arranged as 'tha'.

2. Sentences with the words jumbled; the child rewrites the sentence with the words in the correct order. Again a picture is needed as a clue.

3. A card containing about four small pictures, beside each of which are written two words that differ in only one letter, for example 'mug' and 'rug'. The child selects and writes the word which represents the picture.

4. Pictures accompanied by descriptive words with missing letters, for the child to complete.

5. 'Choose the right words':

A baby dog is called a ——
A baby pig is called a ——
A baby cat is called a ——
A baby duck is called a ——
A baby cow is called a ——
A baby sheep is called a ——

kitten, lamb, puppy, duckling, piglet, calf

Alternatively:

A pin is fat
     thin

A feather is light
     heavy

Coal is black
    green

Or pairing words:

Bread and ——
Knife and ——
Fish and ——
Cup and ——
Bacon and ——
Table and ——

eggs, butter, chair, chips, fork, saucer

It is necessary at this stage for the words to be given at the bottom of the card in order to simplify the child's choice. At a later stage these can be omitted and he must find the words for himself.

6. A picture of a mouse: 'Write 6 more words beginning with "m".'

7. Rhyming words: 'Write some words that rhyme with "can".'

8. A large picture accompanied by some simply worded question cards relating to the picture.

9. Nonsense cards: a picture with two or three phrases or sentences, only one of which is a sensible description.

10. Story cards: most of the writing which children do during

this stage is still in the nature of 'reporting', on either an immediate activity or recent personal experience, or on an aspect of a topic which has caught the child's interest and which can be simply described in the amount of writing which his skill allows. There is, however, a place for a few suggestions for writing which he might like to take up if he is disinclined to write about what he has been doing.

He is not quite ready for flights of fancy and wholly imaginative composition, so suggestions on story cards should generally concern the kind of things he knows about, for example write about your family, what you would like to be when you grow up, playing in the snow, a fire-engine rushing by, your dog, your friend's dog, playing football, your birthday. Centres of interest can move outside the child's experience because they are supported by information and ideas and visual materials supplied by the teacher and other children; but 'stories' draw entirely upon the child's own intellectual resources, and for this reason they are still likely to arise primarily from personal experience.

A picture on a story card, connected with the suggested subject, adds interest and is a source of ideas.

By no means all the children will reach the end of the stage described in this chapter before they leave the First School. However, those who do have made a useful start in learning to read and write. They have mastered the initial skills on which so much of their learning is dependent and, given good teaching, there is no need to fear for their continued progress. They are well on the way to becoming literate.

Chapter 13

The Fluent Readers in the Classroom

THE CHILDREN

Though they are unlikely to be in the majority (unless environmental and school conditions are exceptionally favourable) quite a number of children reach the stage of being able to read fluently while they are still in the First School. This achievement represents a notable landmark in a child's life, because once the technical skill of reading ceases to present any difficulty a whole range of learning is open to him of which he could not have much more than a glimpse before. It affects his progress in many other intellectual skills, since the lack of reading fluency unavoidably limits his horizons in many directions. For these and other reasons children who have reached this stage have changed a good deal since the days when they were reaching tentatively towards a mastery of the printed word.

They are, on the whole, much more sure of themselves. This does not mean that they never experience uncertainties and frustrations, or that children who are by nature anxious or quiet or timid cease to display these characteristics just because they can read. They do, however, tend to recognise that they have accomplished something which is intellectually satisfying and which gives them some degree of parity with the adults around them who have long made use of written language while they could not. There is no doubt that the child who can read effortlessly and confidently feels more grown-up and secure in the social as well as the learning situations of his home and school life.

It is true, of course, that these children have matured.

Generally speaking they are older, they are very used to school, and their manipulative skills let them down less often so that there are more things, apart from reading, that they can do quite well. They have experienced intellectual success and they have a certain standing in the eyes of their peers. They can, however, be subjected now to new and perhaps uncomfortable pressures. Because they have achieved intellectual success, and because they are now equipped with a tool which should help them to advance in many areas of learning, too much can sometimes be expected of them. The fact that they can read the mathematics assignment does not necessarily give them the mathematical understanding to know what they are supposed to do. This is not a trap into which the experienced teacher will fall, but it is not so very difficult for the teacher at the outset of her career to expect of the good reader in the First School a degree of all round ability which in fact may not yet be manifest.

Home pressures, too, can fall quite heavily upon this child, especially in the home where there is interest amounting to over-anxiety about his progress, an excessive concern that he shall 'get on' and be successful. Certainly these may be exceptional cases; but we must not assume that because a child can read fluently he has no intellectual or emotional problems which to him are taxing. He is, despite it all, still a young child. Nevertheless he is equipped with the means which permit his learning—and his teaching—to assume wider dimensions.

We recognise that some children will reach the stage of reading fluently while they are still chronologically and maturationally much younger than the 'average' child at the same level of intellectual development. Our demands on these children, in terms of their total school achievement, must take account of this. The very young fluent reader is, after all, a very young fluent reader. His emotional and physical resources may be no greater than those of his non-reading friends, and while we take steps to sustain his advance in reading we cannot help but be aware of his limitations in other ways. He may, for example, experience difficulty in causing his pencil to write a recognisable word, or in cutting out a picture. He will, however, be very bored if his reading skill is not put to use. This is one of the children who can benefit so much from the individual teaching which the more fluid modern approach permits.

READING: OBJECTIVES AND POSSIBILITIES

We have already observed that, with all 'stages' in the progress of learning, the line of demarcation between one stage and the next is very blurred. The 'advancing readers' do not become the 'fluent readers' overnight. But for the purposes of classroom practice it will be assumed in this chapter that these children have finally crossed the frontier—and the teacher will use her own judgement as to when a child can be considered to have done so. We are therefore now dealing with children who have reached the stage of reading fluently in the sense that they can decipher, without any but perhaps a momentary difficulty, virtually all they meet in print. One class of children established their own yardstick; the magic moment had arrived when they could read upside down! It was doubtless as good a criterion to them as anything the teacher, with a battery of tests and assessment techniques, might have devised.

At any rate we will assume that the technical skill of reading is now securely established; and this brings us to the really vital issue which must now concern us: the development of reading skill for purposes of pleasure, intellectual enrichment and information.

Some of this will come from encouraging the child to read as many and as varied a selection of books as possible. In adult life, however, we employ different reading techniques according to the nature of our reading matter and the purpose for which we are reading it. When we read for information, for example, our object is to extract and comprehend the informational content of the material and often we need to be able to do this with the least possible expenditure of time. If for pleasure and relaxation we read something 'light' like a detective story, we read it quickly and with the minimum of intellectual effort because our object is to unfold the mystery and reach the solution—just because we enjoy doing so. If, on the other hand, as Jane Austen addicts we are reading one of her novels, we will probably read it slowly and literally word for word, for the sheer delight of savouring the language which gives us so much pleasure.

Once a child can read really fluently he can begin developing these varying techniques. It is outside the scope of this book to discuss in detail all that a teacher may do to encourage the effective growth of these different reading skills; it is in any case a process that continues far beyond the First School years. However, some notes on the positive steps that the teacher may take at this early stage to initiate such development may serve a useful purpose.

1. Encourage the children to begin reading books critically. Ask them to write, *sometimes*, a review of a book they have read, but give them some guidance on what to consider when they are doing this. Make a small folder containing two or three sets of questions which become progressively more demanding.

  (i) What was the book about?
 (ii) What did you like best in it?
(iii) What did you like least?
 (iv) Were there any words that you especially liked?
  (v) Why did you like them?

Later questions can ask more of the child: 'Were you sorry to come to the end of the book, or did you have to try hard to go on reading it? Why?' If the book was read for information: 'Did it tell you what you wanted to know? Did it explain clearly?' If the child has no guidance as to the kind of questions he should ask himself when reviewing a book he will hardly know where to begin and may well never get around to doing it. A class book in which the reviews are pasted will encourage others to follow suit.

2. When asking a child specifically to extract information from a book, give him some questions to which he must find the answers and some assignments to undertake as a result of his reading, for example 'What did Stone Age men live in? How did they get their food? Draw a Stone Age family, showing how they lived.'

3. Ask a group of children to read a particular book and organise a debate at which they discuss it.

4. Encourage children to study words. Ask them to make a list

of new words as they come across them and have a short discussion session now and again to consider some of the new words they have found. What do they mean? Are they like (or are they derived from) any other words that they know? Do they know any more words which mean the same thing? Do any of these words have more than one meaning?

This kind of session should be short and informal, the object being to encourage children to study words, to begin looking for derivations, to develop an interest in words and to enlarge their vocabularies. It should not, and it need not, be undertaken as a dull word exercise in which new words are simply listed and learned. This would probably defeat the object, since it would be more likely to kill rather than to foster interest in new words.

5. Try to develop an interest in the sound of words. Think of some onomatopoeic words; make up some onomatopoeic words; write a poem using some of them and see what it sounds like. Are there any other words which would have sounded better?

6. Begin using direct methods to develop speed in word recognition, such as rapid flash card work.

7. Extend the children's phonic skills, both for decoding and for encoding words. *Teach* them the common vowel and consonant combinations which they can now accommodate (see Appendix D). Make use of games like those in the *Programmed Reading Kit*[1] and indeed any other reading games which you may devise.[2]

Help the children to assemble longer and more complex words that are phonically regular. Encourage them to learn how to spell some of the everyday irregular words that they meet frequently, like *said, was, could, know, because*.

8. Teach them the alphabetic names of letters; many children will in any case be using these by now, because they are more 'grown up' and often quicker to say than the sound equivalents they used to use. Teach them to say the alphabet; they will not experience any difficulty in learning it by heart and it is handy to know the alphabet.

9. Apart from requiring the children to read for particular

[1] D. H. Stott, op. cit.
[2] For some ideas about reading games and other useful aids, see John M. Hughes, *Aids to Reading* (London, Evans, 1970).

purposes, do permit—and encourage—them to read during the day just for pleasure, with no strings attached. Try to spare a moment to take an interest in the book a child is reading and have a word with him about it.

10. Do make the time to give some thought to children's literature and select with care the stories and the poetry that you read for them. This will help them more than anything else to develop taste and discrimination in their reading without feeling that you are censoring what they read. Suggest titles that they might try to borrow from the public library, but do not expect them never to read 'rubbish'. They are bound to do so in any case, and if they should learn to be critical of even one bad book more good than harm will result from their reading it.[3]

WRITING: OBJECTIVES AND POSSIBILITIES

Once children can write with ease the teacher can begin training them to leaven quantity with quality. Her aim should be to help them to recognise quality and to absorb it into their own writing rather than to attempt direct instruction on what quality, or lack of it, may be. Much of this absorption will come from the children's own reading and here we see how closely the growth of reading and writing skills are interlocked. However, the teacher must help to promote the child's assimilation of quality from his reading, and this can best be done by means of a personal and conversational interchange of opinion concerning particular aspects of something he has written.

Teacher and child can, for example, consider a descriptive word he has used and together try to think of any other words which might on another occasion be substituted. They can ask themselves whether the addition of an adjective or an adverb in a particular sentence would have heightened the atmosphere or strengthened the meaning. They can look at some of the joining 'ands' to see whether an alternative might not sound

[3] As an introduction to the subject of children's literature, read Joan E. Cass, *Literature and the Young Child* (London, Longman, 1967). This is an excellent and informative little book, with a good bibliography of stories, verse anthologies, periodicals, etc. which are suitable and enjoyable for young children.

better. They can read a short passage from a book and listen to what happens to the flow of reading when there is a comma, and then read some of the child's writing, listening for the slight pause or change of intonation which implies a comma like the one they found in the book. It is not suggested that this should be done with every piece of the child's writing. This would be neither practicable nor desirable. But an occasional conversation of this kind does a great deal to help the child to be aware of quality—to reinforce his assimilation of it from his own reading and to enable him to begin applying it, at least some of the time, in the language and structure he uses when he writes.

It is from this sort of incidental teaching that the rules of punctuation are most easily learned, including quotation marks (they indicate your two lips—or one mouth—which you open to say something and which you close again when you have finished saying it). It is also from this kind of conversation that many of the common spelling mistakes can be corrected without fuss—'You have spelt "said" the wrong way. See if you can find it in a book and come and tell me the right way.' This is much more likely to help the child to spell it correctly the next time than if it is simply altered when his writing is marked. Again one does not suggest that this can be done every time; but it underlines the value of the conversational teaching that can take place from time to time if the teacher is aware of the possibilities and sets out to make use of them whenever she can.

As the children's writing skill develops they will need to draw upon a greater variety of sources in order to exercise their skill. Some will engage, with pleasure and satisfaction, in imaginative writing; others will be more at ease with a factual or informative approach; some children will prefer to write almost entirely about the pursuit of a current personal interest in insects or aeroplanes or whatever it might be, or about activities directly connected with the development of a project. It is extremely important, however, that the teacher should recognise the continued existence of the need, with many children, for help and ideas with what they can write about. It is quite erroneous to suppose that because children are skilful enough to write fluently they now have an unlimited capacity for thinking of something to write about at the drop of a hat. Very few children—or adults for that matter—possess this capacity, and they can become quite worried and irritated by the unqualified instruction to 'write about it'—whether 'it' is a visit to the police station or a project about Egyptians. It is part of the teacher's responsibility to make available to children, advanced though their writing skill may be, a sufficient range of subject material to satisfy a variety of interest, temperament, mood and purpose.

In this connection there is one further point to which the teacher should give attention. Children at this stage should not be asked to write a story every day. If they are, interest in writing, and particularly in the development of quality, can very easily be threatened. If children are to make the effort to produce a story or other piece of writing which is to be something more than the fulfilment of a limited immediate objective, they must be given the time and the opportunity to sustain this effort and bring it to fruition. More often than not it cannot be accomplished in a day.

One approach that can have very productive results is to make available, perhaps in a manilla wall pocket, coloured sugar paper folders and a supply of writing paper, to which the child may help himself as his story or whatever he is engaged in progresses. He need not hand this in until it is complete. It may take several days, or even a week or two, before the 'story' is finished. It is then stapled into one of the sugar paper folders, the title and the name of the 'author' written on the front and the cover decorated if the child wishes. He has then written a 'book', which he has been given time to write, and for the completion of which he has had a strong incentive. It is remarkably satisfying, when you are seven or eight, to have written a book, which looks like a book and is respected as a book. Moreover, it provides tangible evidence of the sum of effort that otherwise would have been dispersed in little bits of unrelated, and often unfinished, writing that cannot be put together in a very rewarding way. For those children who cannot sustain such a prolonged effort, a book of 'short stories' compiled over a period of time can offer similar satisfaction.

The technical skill

There is now a place for handwriting lessons, in which the children are required to achieve as high a standard as possible in letter formation, in even spacing and in the general production and appearance of their writing. Such lessons are more beneficial if they are short and well directed—say about twenty minutes or so once a week. It is quite useful to concentrate on one letter in each lesson, finishing with a short phrase in which it appears several times and possibly with a writing pattern related to the shape of the letter.

It is most important that insistence on this standard should be limited to handwriting lessons, and that it should not extend to the children's personal writing. If it does, the quality of their written language is likely to suffer because they will have to give undue attention to how they write rather than what they write. However, the skill and practice derived from handwriting lessons will, in time, spill over into the child's normal writing, and an improvement in the standard of the technical skill will come, almost unnoticed. If there are no handwriting lessons (which can be conducted perfectly pleasantly and informally) unnecessarily poor handwriting will be perpetuated for far longer than is necessary and it is difficult to see how this can be justified.

The question of making fair copies of written work, for display purposes, is a bit controversial. If, as sometimes happens, everything that is to be displayed has to be rewritten in a beautiful hand, with a decorative border, too much of a child's time and effort (which could be better spent in other ways) is wasted. Interest can be dissipated, too, by the knowledge that the wretched thing will in any case have to be written twice. For a special display, where the main purpose is to exhibit examples of things which are visually attractive or even beautiful, samples of rewritten 'best writing' are justifiable. For other purposes, children's writing should be displayed in its natural state. As in everything else, there is a moderate line between extremes.

APPARATUS

At this level apparatus can, if the teacher wishes, provide additional aids for the development of reading and writing skills. It is still important, however, that the *purpose* of such apparatus is well considered. If it does not serve a particular purpose, which cannot be better served in some other way, then the teacher's time is wasted in making it and the child's time is wasted in using it. A short selection of the kind of apparatus that can be of value is therefore given below under 'purpose' headings.

For the development of phonic skills
1. Write six words beginning with 'cr'. Write a sentence using some of these words.
2. Make words by adding letters to the beginning of
ear, eel, eat, ate.
See how many words you can make.
(Similarly, letters can be added to the end of suitable vowel and consonant combinations, or inserted in the middle.)

3. Change the first letter of these words to 'b' and write a sentence using each one.

cat, melt, dear, cake.

For developing accuracy in the use of words
1. Copy these words and find the ones that are missing.

I jump	I do
I am ——	I am ——
I have ——	I have ——
I go	I write
I am ——	I am ——
I have ——	I have ——

2. Copy these sentences, choosing the right word for the one that is missing.

no or know: I —— a boy called Tom.
                  There is —— school on Saturdays.

here or hear: My pencil is ——.
                    I can —— a noise.

by or buy: We —— bread at the baker's shop.
                    I watched a train going ——.

3. Try and write these sentences differently.

I seen a big dog.
We had fish an chips.
Tony and Ann is painting a picture.

For training children to look at and listen to words
1. Take the last letter off each word. Draw a picture of the word that is left.

many   sunk   cart   bush

2. Write a list of words that rhyme with

mat   bed   ink   log

3. Write down all the words you can make from

c a l e n d a r s

For the use and extension of vocabulary
1. Write these sentences, using other words instead of the ones with lines under them.

Susan is wearing a nice dress.
That tree is very big.
Coal is as black as ink.

2. Write some words which are the opposite of

fat   black   heavy   tall   rough

3. Write as many words as you can think of to describe

a thunderstorm
a piece of velvet
Guy Fawkes night

For the development of comprehension in reading and interest in finding information
1. A card for a practical task (for example making a cardboard crown), giving written instructions on how to do it.

2. Small assignment books, containing questions to which children must find the answers and tasks for them to perform, for example one about dogs: 'Make a list of different kinds of dogs. Describe your own dog, or your friend's dog. What do dogs need to make them healthy and happy? Do a painting of a dog, or make one from clay. Some dogs can be trained to do special jobs—try and find out what these dogs can do: a sheep dog; a St Bernard; a husky.' These questions would appear on separate pages in the assignment book.

3. Cards connected with finding information or undertaking assignments related to the current project or topic.

For ideas of things to write about

1. Story cards. These can include anything which may capture a child's interest or stimulate his imagination. A really interesting picture may be sufficient. For some children it may be helpful to add one or two suggestions, such as a picture of a castle. 'This is a castle where a lord and lady lived long ago. Write a story about what happened when another lord came with his soldiers and tried to capture it.' Sometimes it helps to give the first few words of a sentence, breaking it off at the point when an idea is suggested, for example a picture of a child looking at the sea: 'Sally was by the sea one day when suddenly she saw a. . . .'

2. Pictures which present opportunities for self-expression in a form other than writing stories appeal to some children, for example a veteran car: 'Which would you rather have, a veteran car or a new one? Pretend that you have a car of your own and write about what you would like to do with it and where you would like to go.'

3. The sound of words may suggest a story. 'Say these words to yourself: crashed, splashed, flashed, dashed. Say them again and see if they make you think of a story to write.'

There is no doubt at all that there are children, still in the First School, whose reading and writing skill is capable of development to the extent that has been suggested in this chapter. Every school may not have these children, and some may have only a few; but children who have the good fortune to possess the advantages which make reading and writing of this standard possible at a comparatively early age need the intellectual sustenance on which they can flourish. If the demands made upon them match their capacity, the extent of their advance can be really quite surprising.[4]

[4] Book I of the series *Let's Imagine* by Wallace Eyre (Oxford, Blackwell, 1967) contains many attractive and stimulating ideas for the development of children's spoken and written language, appropriate to this stage.

Chapter 14

The Children with Reading Difficulties

This chapter does not attempt to cover the whole field of remedial techniques in the teaching of reading as they may apply during the First School years. This is a highly specialised area of study, which has been the subject over the years of extensive investigation and much dedicated practice by teachers who are especially concerned with helping the backward reader. It would be wholly inappropriate, in a practical exposition of the initial teaching of reading in the First School, to imply that it is possible in a few pages to equip the teacher with all that she really needs to know about remedying reading failure in young children. It is therefore necessary to define the terms within which it is proposed here to identify the problem, and to suggest measures that may help children who are experiencing more than average difficulty in learning to read.

As we all know, there are degrees of reading failure, ranging from total inability at the end of the First School to interpret the printed word, to difficulty in mastering the basic skill with sufficient fluency and comprehension to support comfortably the child's general progress. The causes of these degrees of reading failure range equally widely, from those which are physiological or severely psychological in origin to those which are not so disabling that the teacher who makes it her business may not hope to contribute appreciably towards modifying their effect. Tansley defines this last type of failure as that which is 'normally cured by the use of good, normal teaching for the individual child because it is not due to any physical or psychological abnormality and hardly deserves the description of acute disability'.[1]

[1] A. E. Tansley, *Reading and Remedial Reading* (London, Routledge & Kegan Paul, 1967), p. 130.

It is not with the cause and effect of severe reading disability that we are here concerned. Modern medical and educational views increasingly support the belief that children who are afflicted with any kind of disability, whether intellectual, emotional or physical, should, whenever possible, be educated in the ordinary school. This applies most particularly when they are very young because, except in really pronounced cases, it is not always easy at this time to determine the precise nature of the disability or to know how far good teaching in the ordinary school will of itself help the child more than his removal to a sheltered and specialist learning environment. This means that the teacher in the First School may certainly have children in her class suffering from quite severe disabilities, including those which affect their capacity to learn to read.

Some of these children will not learn to read while they are still in the First School, and others will make a start. It is for them, however, that the teacher needs to apply more specialised diagnostic and remedial techniques than can possibly be dealt with here, and no attempt will be made to give superficial advice on the subject. The teacher must turn to specialist studies for help and guidance in this area of her teaching.

Apart from these children, however, there are those who experience more difficulty than most in the acquisition of reading skill. Sometimes the reasons for this are not hard to identify —emotional disturbance, poor health, linguistic disadvantage, intellectual limitation—and the common sense as well as some of the pedagogical measures which a teacher may take to mitigate the effects of these disadvantages have been discussed elsewhere in this book. However, there still remain detailed and practical considerations which arise with regard to these children and their day-to-day life in the classroom, and the purpose of this chapter is to try to assist the teacher in identifying some of the ways in which she may be able to help them.

POTENTIAL CASES OF READING FAILURE

It is a truism to say that in any area of learning prevention of failure is more effective than any measures which may be taken to cure it once the failure is manifest. Truism or not, it may well be especially applicable to reading since success in so much else depends upon the ability to read. This being so, the teacher needs to be alert to *potential* cases of reading failure or difficulty.

The main factors which appear to affect a child's ability to learn to read are well enough known. The adverse effects of some of them may be counteracted by the teacher; she may at least alleviate them, even if she cannot eradicate them. The child, for example, who suffers from prolonged or frequent absence from school is potentially a strong candidate for reading failure. If the teacher can so organise her time as to give this child some extra, personal, individual help when he returns to school, she may well be doing far more for him than can be done in all the hours a remedial teacher may spend later on, once he has fallen so far behind that he clearly qualifies as 'a child with reading difficulties'.

We know that this is a counsel of perfection. We know that time is one of the most severely rationed of the commodities that the teacher has at her disposal. We know that many causes of reading difficulty are much more complex and less easy to isolate and deal with than the example quoted. Nevertheless it remains true that the undramatic rescue of one potential reading failure must stand high on the list of priorities to which a teacher's time and attention can be given. It is at least an identifiable and practical contribution that she can make in tackling one possible cause of reading difficulty.

THE IMPORTANCE OF THE DIAGNOSIS OF READING DIFFICULTY[2]

If the teacher is to attack the problem at its source she must quite explicitly direct herself towards trying to isolate its causes. There is a great deal of evidence to support the view that any marked degree of reading failure is seldom due to just *one* reason. Nearly always there are several adverse influences which are reacting to the child's disadvantage. It follows that the teacher must give close personal attention to the one individual child who she has reason to believe may be at risk in learning to read and try to understand as much as

[2] For some helpful information on 'Identifying the Problem', see A. E. Tansley, op. cit., pp. 72–80.

she can about his circumstances, his temperament, his hopes
and fears, his family, his intellectual capacity as far as this
may be evident, his health—indeed, she must try to learn
everything she can about him. With the knowledge she thus
gains about this one child she is in a position to try to make
an assessment of the measures that may be needed to help
him with his difficulties. For some of these measures she will
need outside help, from the medical officer, the educational
psychologist, the welfare officer, the child's parents, and through
the head teacher she can seek this assistance. Some of the
measures, however, are those she can take within her own
classroom, by making special provision for the child, by trying
to establish as helpful a relationship with him as possible, by
adjusting her demands upon him to take account of emotional
or temperamental disturbance. She will have no magic wand
to wave for this child, and she may have several such children
in her class. But she is more likely to be able to help them
with their reading problems if she is as fully acquainted as
possible with all the factors which she may need to take into
account. The diagnosis of potential and actual causes of reading difficulty, though far from easy and often necessarily in-
complete, is an essential and constructive step that the teacher
can take in helping the child to avert the consequences of real
reading failure.

THE MODIFICATION OF A SENSE OF FAILURE

When a child is falling behind in learning to read, he knows
he is falling behind. We would often like to persuade ourselves
that he does not know, or at least that if he does know he takes
it philosophically and does not mind. It is superficially true
that some forms of practice may delay his realisation of the
fact for a little while; if, for example, no reading scheme is
used in the class there is not such an obvious source of comparison by which he can measure his progress against that of
others. This, however, is only a temporary palliative. At best it
merely defers the sense of failure, and at worst it may obscure
the fact of his reading weakness to the teacher as well as the
child, at the very time when remedial action may be especially
valuable.

It may also be true that some children mind more than others. It is, however, very doubtful that any child does not mind at all. Of course he would prefer to find learning to read as easy as other children seem to find it, and it is surely wishful thinking on our part to assume that if a child appears not to care he in fact does not suffer from being unable to do what others can.

However, even though we may not be able to prevent a child from recognising that his level of reading ability is below that of most children in the class, there is a certain amount that the teacher can do to support his confidence and mitigate his sense of failure at this early stage. Perhaps the first and most important element in this situation is her own attitude. Vital though it is that the child shall learn to read, she must do all she can not to let him feel that other things which he may perhaps do quite well are not also important. In concentrating on trying to diagnose the causes of his difficulty, she must pursue a tactful course. She must avoid giving him the impression that she has uncovered a mortal weakness which will consume him unless the emergency squad is called in. Her extra help must be matter-of-fact and treated as something quite ordinary, while at the same time she must let the child realise that she is there to help him and is in fact doing so. It is not a particularly easy balance to maintain, but the teacher has to try. The position is further complicated by the fact that there are children whose lack of progress is due in large part to lack of effort. In attempting to diagnose the causes of reading difficulty, she must try to decide whether lack of effort is a major factor and whether she should put pressure on the child to try harder. This, again, is not an easy judgement but the teacher's strongest safeguard is the effort she has made to learn all she can about the child. It is on the basis of this knowledge that her course of action must be determined.

In the case of the child whose confidence the teacher knows she must try to support, there are some positive steps she can take. She must take every opportunity for drawing attention to his success, however limited, in the other areas of classroom activity. If he can even be one of the best at tidying up or taking a message it can do much for his self-esteem. The important thing is that the teacher should be able to give this child the impression that she depends on him for his skill and reliability in performing a particular task.

It can all be made to sound so easy in theory. The sad fact is that nature is not often just. The child who lacks ability or who has many disadvantageous influences working against him is not automatically compensated for this by being given outstanding qualities of practical skill or dependability. In practice it is so often hard to find a way in which a child who is failing can be made to feel successful, particularly as the teacher must be careful not to do this so obviously that it is patently false to the child himself as well as to everyone else. It is, however, one of the ways in which a child's self-confidence can be nurtured and if the teacher can apply the principle on even the most modest scale she will be doing something towards helping him to feel that he is not a total failure.

As far as the practical use of reading materials is concerned it often helps if the teacher can give the child a completely fresh start. A change of reading scheme, to one that he does not associate with failure, can make an appreciable difference. A new range of purpose made apparatus, designed to give him the experience appropriate to an earlier stage while taking account of his more advanced level of maturity and his changing interests can also help. If in the class there are younger children, at an earlier level of development, the older child who cannot read can be permitted to 'help' one of the younger children with his reading material; in this way he can himself regress to an earlier stage without loss of face. Some of the modern teaching machines, too, can be of real assistance to such a child. The 'Language Master', for example, may be used to provide material which is especially tailored to individual need. Such machines, however, are very expensive, and it is not to be supposed that every school can afford to buy one to meet the special needs of a small number of children. However, should the provision of a teaching machine be possible, it offers one of the means by which additional help can be given to the child with reading difficulties.[3]

In giving the child extra help in the classroom, or in making

[3] For a clear and informative summary of the 'Hardware for Reading', see Donald and Louise Moyle, *Modern Innovations in the Teaching of Reading*, chap. 5.

special provision for him, the teacher's aim must be to try to offer him the chance of immediate success, however limited this may be. The special material must therefore be designed to be *within his capacity at that time*, subsequently increasing in difficulty in very small steps and with clear and obvious short-term goals. If the child can have an objective that is within his reach and can measure his progress each time he achieves his objective, he is likely to be more strongly motivated to try and get there. If, on the other hand, rapid and measurable success is too remote from his grasp, even a comparatively moderate degree of reading failure can quickly assume almost giant proportions and the seeds of an acute problem have been sown.

ACTION IN THE FIRST SCHOOL

It has generally been the practice to defer direct remedial help for the slow reader until he is in the junior school. By no means all children have learned to read by the time they leave the infant school, particularly those who are the youngest in the age group and have been in school only about two years. However, although it is acknowledged that many of these children have not yet had long enough to master the skill, they have all too frequently been given insufficient help in the first junior year because the initial teaching of reading has not, in the past, been really regarded as part of the junior teacher's job. When children have reached the second junior year and are still unable to read, they have been classed as 'backward readers' and in enlightened schools have been given remedial help. By this time, of course, their sense of failure is acute and their progress in many other areas of learning seriously affected.

This situation has been changing in recent years. In some junior schools active help with reading is now made available from the first year, and the advent of the First School in any case defers the child's transfer from the environment in which teachers are well accustomed to initial teaching techniques. Moreover, more attention is now being given to the advisability of attacking the problem directly and of giving the child special help at a much earlier stage, in an attempt to prevent reading failure instead of waiting until it has happened and then trying to 'cure' it.

There is much sense in this view, but if efforts to anticipate and prevent reading failure are to be successful First Schools must be equipped to tackle the problem. It is just not sufficient to leave the children there a year longer and assume that the First School teacher of a class of thirty or forty can perform miracles with the slow readers simply because she was 'infant trained'. This would merely transfer the problem from one school to another but would do little to solve it.

Additional professional help *must* be made available, as it now is in some junior schools, so that the children who need it can be given extra assistance in small groups. This implies the recruitment of a 'remedial teacher', at least on a part-time basis, but there is a great deal to be said for the class teacher taking the small group while the visiting teacher takes the rest of the class for part of its normal day's activities. It is surely the children in need of help who are also most in need of continuity of teaching and above all of the opportunity for their 'remedial' reading to carry over from the rest of their learning and to continue to have direct reference to it when they are back in the classroom. If these children disappear at intervals with another teacher 'to be taught to read', not only is their failure made more explicit but also their reading activity is isolated from much else that they do. It is difficult to see how this can be in their best interest.

If the principle of prevention being better than cure is to be applied, perhaps quite early in the First School, the question arises of identifying the children who are to be given the additional help. There is, after all, no problem of identification once the child's failure is made clear by the fact that most of the others have succeeded in learning to read. It is to the much earlier signs of weakness—not necessarily *failure*—that the teacher will need to attend. It is much harder to detect weakness in reading which if left unstrengthened may well amount, perhaps avoidably, to real failure at a later stage.

The child may simply be slower to start, but once he begins he is as much at ease with learning to read as anyone else. All this child needs is the opportunity to move at his own pace and to come to terms comfortably with new learning situations. He does not need 'remedial' reading help. But how is the teacher to know whether or not the child is just a slow starter?

We do not, in the classroom, meet clinically remote situations which the teacher has to judge in isolation from the children with whom she spends her day. After all, she knows them as people and the child himself is there, with his conversation and his personality and his reactions, to guide her judgement. With her knowledge of the child she may observe, *if she is alert to them*, signs of difficulty, for example poor visual discrimination (more confusion over the identification of differences and similarities than most of the others seem to experience), poor auditory discrimination (this may become apparent as phonic training progresses), anxiety about reading (the child may try too hard and become distressed when he makes a mistake, or he may try to escape from reading activity if he can find a way of avoiding it), lack of adequate linguistic resources of his own, poor motor co-ordination. These are some of the common sense criteria which the observant teacher can apply in judging the individual reactions of her children when she is teaching them to read, and they may lead her to consider how she may best help the child who appears to exhibit some weakness.

To begin with, then, the First School teacher should try to help *potential* cases of reading weakness, as suggested earlier in this chapter. As reading begins, she will also be alert to possible signs of weakness such as those which have just been indicated. Some of the extra help that these situations require can be given by the teacher in her normal dealings with the class; but there is no question whatever that if some additional professional help could be provided, really effective preventive measures could now be taken. Time could be spent with a small group, with activities which will develop their language skills; more personal attention could be given for a little while to those who need help with materials designed to strengthen poor visual discrimination. This is not remedial teaching in the conventional sense. It is just ordinary everyday practice, but the need is for the practice to be so organised that it is possible for the teacher to underpin her day-to-day teaching with the reinforcement from which some children at this early stage can so greatly benefit.

It may be argued that with the individual teaching methods employed in modern practice this underpinning goes on anyway, as a matter of course. Certainly it does, up to a point; but it is idle to suppose that the teacher with a class of thirty or more, however modern and individual her approach, can really effectively undertake the additional preventive measures that the apparently or potentially weak reader needs.

In the present situation, where part-time professional help is not normally available at an early stage in the First School, all that the teacher can do is to be as knowledgeable about her children as possible, to train herself to be as alert as she can to signs of reading weakness, and to try to organise her time by any means in her power to give these children a little extra help—the common sense help rather than, in this particular context, the specialised remedial teaching that is needed by the child whose reading disability is severe. She may take comfort from the fact that *any* direct help she can give to the weaker reader contributes to the modification of his future problem. She must not let herself become discouraged by the lack of obviously successful results. Her most sincere and conscientious efforts may seem to achieve little that is immediately apparent. If, however, she can view the slower child's progress over the length of a term and note that he has moved forward rather than made no progress at all, she will know that her efforts are bearing fruit and that the help she is giving the child is yielding positive and measurable results.[4]

[4] Further reading is essential to the teacher who is concerned to help the child with reading difficulties. A very good basic book on the subject is A. E. Tansley, *Reading and Remedial Reading*, to which reference has already been made.

Chapter 15

Conclusion

In defining the aims of the curriculum of the primary school, Dearden writes:

Once [the child] has learned to read, he can read to learn. . . . Being able to read is a crucial condition of education itself. . . . Furthermore, a child who cannot read is necessarily a child who cannot write, so that any kind of creative or factual writing is barred to the non-reading child.[1]

No one will dispute the validity of this view; but there is lack of agreement on the extent to which teaching, in the direct sense of the word, can be responsible for helping to achieve the aim that it expresses.

The theme of this book is that the overwhelming majority of children will not learn to read and write effectively unless they are taught, skilfully, to do so. We cannot avoid a sense of unease at the conclusions of the latest report on reading standards, of children aged eleven and fifteen, which suggest that the progressive improvement in reading attainment which emerged from the 1961 survey has not been maintained in the last decade.[2] Despite the reservations which the authors of the report made about their findings, no one who is concerned with teaching children to read or with training teachers to do so will treat the conclusions of the survey with complacency. Success in learning to read and write is too important.

It is undoubtedly true that reading is often well taught and that when this happens it receives little or no publicity. We

[1] R. F. Dearden, *The Philosophy of Primary Education* (London, Routledge & Kegan Paul, 1968), p. 87.
[2] K. B. Start and B. K. Wells, *The Trend of Reading Standards* (National Foundation for Educational Research, 1972). Survey commissioned by the Department of Education and Science, and conducted between June 1970 and March 1971.

know, however, that it is not always well taught in schools and that the teacher is not always adequately trained to set about her task. It would help us all if we could point to a method which is known to be the best for children in order that they may learn to read; but unfortunately there is no such blueprint for success. Nevertheless there are some indications which merit our attention.

From the welter of research and investigations into the teaching of reading which has been undertaken in recent years, two conclusions seem to emerge with clarity:

(i) It is not possible to isolate any *one* method or approach which is inherently superior to all others and which, of itself, offers the best chance of success in teaching children to read.

(ii) The most important single factor in the whole process is the skill of the teacher. This outweighs all other elements in the attainment of the ultimate result.

These conclusions are supported by many writers and a number of independent studies. As far back as 1954, in a summary of research findings by Yates, the assumed superiority of 'activity' as opposed to 'formal' methods or of 'phonic' compared with 'look-and-say' was shown to be without foundation when judged by research evidence. With regard to the 'activity' versus the 'formal' approach, the teacher who adhered rigidly to either was seldom found. 'In practice, most teachers offer a judicious mixture of the two methods and the extreme stereotypes are rarely encountered.' (One wonders, however, if this is quite as true today as it was in the 1950s.) Yates suggested that, in the long term, activity methods 'if efficiently and enthusiastically undertaken' yielded results 'at least as impressive as those produced by the best systematic methods'. On the other hand, 'if one judges the relative merits of the two methods in terms of the scores obtained by the children at the end of, say, two years on an objective test of reading attainments, the formal methods must be regarded as superior'; he adds, however, that if one is concerned with 'the broader aspects of development—for instance, the children's interest in reading as distinct from their prowess within the narrow range of skills measured by the objective tests—this superiority may not be so apparent.' He concludes that 'some compromise between these two approaches would seem to be a sensible procedure.'

Referring to the comparative merits of 'phonic' and 'look-and-say', Yates suggests that

... three main conclusions can be drawn from the investigations that have been carried out.

(a) No method appears to be equally effective with different groups of children. ...

(b) No method appears to be equally effective when applied by different teachers. ...

(c) Different methods promote development in different directions. ...

The eclectic approach is therefore soundly based. 'To introduce children to reading by means of the "look-and-say" method and then, at a later stage, to encourage systematic phonic analysis and word building would seem to be the best procedure to adopt in the light of the evidence so far available.'[3]

Despite the fact that this was written some time ago, it is quoted because more recent research is not substantially at variance with Yates's main conclusions that a 'mixed' approach is the most likely to harness the advantages and counteract the disadvantages inherent in any one way of teaching. '. . . no one approach is so distinctly better in all situations and respects than the others that it should be considered the one best method and the one to be used exclusively.'[4] Dr Margaret Clark, reflecting upon studies which have been undertaken in this country and elsewhere, makes the same point and adds another.

Investigations into the effect of different teaching methods on levels of reading skills have all come to the same conclusion:

[3] Alfred Yates, Officer-in-charge, Research Programme, N.F.E.R., 'The Teaching of Reading from the Researcher's Point of View', in *Child Education* (Autumn Quarterly, 1954).

[4] Bond and Dykstra, reporting on an American study in 1967, quoted by A. Sterl Artley, 'The Teacher Variable in the Teaching of Reading', in *The Reading Teacher*, vol. 23, no. 3 (Dec. 1969).

that though in the short term a new method may appear to improve the standard of reading, in the long-term analysis there is *no single best method* of teaching reading (Chall, 1967; Burt, 1969). Some methods are better for some children; some methods are better used by some teachers. The teacher is the important variable. What is important is that the teacher, whatever method she uses, is aware of the individual members of her class and is prepared to vary the approach to take account of their strengths and weaknesses.[5]

It seems, then, that we have not found the golden key with which the teacher can unlock the door, secure in the knowledge that success is not far away. To carry the analogy a little further, however, it is apparent that the hand which holds the key exercises the influence that matters. *The teacher is the important variable*. The conclusion to be drawn is inescapable.

It is the teacher who exposes the child to the situations from which she hopes he will learn. It is therefore her responsibility to determine what these situations are likely to be and *to ensure that she provides them and that the child makes use of them*. This view is supported by the investigations of Cane and Smithers into infant schools, some of which were found to be more successful than others in the teaching of reading.

What distinguishes the successful from the unsuccessful schools seems quite simple—the existence among their teachers of clearly defined objectives, of a workmanlike approach to their task, of a systematic and planned series of exercises and activities, and of an eclecticism in amalgamating various methods and choosing—at appropriate times—the essential from each. 'Good' teachers and 'good' schools are those which know what they want to do, plan how they intend to do it, and structure the activities of the day and the week accordingly and monitor the progress of their teaching.[6]

Perhaps it is possible to find the teacher who does not believe in teacher direction', but who possesses such outstanding natural gifts that her leadership, her presence and her undirected influence are sufficient to inspire in young children

---

[5] Margaret M. Clark, *Reading Difficulties in Schools* (Harmondsworth, Penguin, 1970), p. 18.
[6] Cane and Smithers, *The Roots of Reading*, p. 7.

the will to learn and the discrimination to select for themselves the means of doing so. Such a teacher, if she exists, is rare indeed. Most of us are made of humbler stuff; and if children are to learn to read and write we must take professionally competent steps to cause them to do so. It is the teacher's skill in identifying these steps and in helping the child along them that in the end makes most children literate.

Appendix A

Some criteria for assessing the suitability of reading schemes

1. Does the main approach of the scheme (i.e. whole word, sentence method, phonic, etc.) reflect your own beliefs and preference? If not, assess how far you can adapt it to do so and what particular measures you can take to modify it.

2. Is the subject matter related to the interests of your children? If not, to what extent does the content allow you to compensate for the deficiency by discussion, by making comparisons, by making supplementary apparatus, etc.?

3. Is the rate of progression satisfactory? Are there supplementary books to modify it for the slow readers? Are the steps between books well graduated?

Look particularly at the first books and judge whether they offer the opportunity for relatively rapid success. Examine the language to see whether it is suitable for the 5-year-old, in sentence structure, word difficulty, word repetition, number of words, etc. Assess whether the words and the way in which they are assembled lend themselves effectively to the use of recognition clues.

Look at the later books. Is the language appropriate and will it have meaning for the children at that stage? Is there enough variety of expression and subject matter to develop language skill? Are the stories sufficiently interesting to sustain the effort of advancing and fluent readers?

4. What is the standard and quality of the illustrations? Is their representation of people up to date? Do they explain the text or obscure it?

5. Is the general standard of production good and suitable for the children? Look at the size and format of books, print, length of line, word arrangement, general layout.

Is the paper of good quality? Are the books well bound and durable?

6. Is there any supplementary material? How do you rate its quality, quantity, effectiveness?

7. Is there a teacher's manual? Is it helpful, practical, explanatory?

Some schemes are more helpful than others for slow readers, some have more to offer children whose progress is rapid. Particular needs such as these often make it necessary for more than one scheme to be available to a teacher and requirements of this kind should be taken into account when choices are made.

Appendix B

Notes on some of the reading schemes

These are schemes in common use, which the writer has either personally experienced in teaching or has had the opportunity of examining in some detail in schools where they are in use.

Gay Way (Macmillan, 1955–66)
Mixed method, but with a strong phonic bias. New edition up to date in content and illustration; goes a long way towards overcoming many of the criticisms of the subject matter in reading schemes. Books attractively produced, and well graded. Useful range of supplementary material.

Happy Trio (Wheaton/Pergamon, 1962)
Very well graded. Mixed method, but early emphasis strongly look-and-say (whole word); phonics introduced rather later. Helpful handbooks to explain the series, and a good range of supplementary material.

Happy Venture (Oliver & Boyd, 1937–70)
Look-and-say to begin with, phonics included from Book 2. Written by Schonell, it was the first scheme to be based on carefully considered psychological principles, with a controlled vocabulary. Illustrations updated in new edition. One of the more effective schemes for slow readers. Good range of supplementary material.

Janet and John (Nisbet, 1949–67)
  Long series: look-and-say.
  Short series: includes phonics.
These can be used independently or interchanged. Very good range of supplementary material. Characters and subject matter rather stereotyped and vocabulary in introductory book is wearisome (an almost inevitable disadvantage with a very carefully controlled vocabulary). Its great merit is that it is extremely well graded and for this reason it is particularly beneficial for slow readers. Later books much more interesting. Illustrations updated in new edition.

Ladybird Key Words Reading Scheme (Wills & Hepworth, 1964)
Mixed method. Small books, satisfying for children to handle, well printed and fully illustrated, produced to the high standard characteristic of all *Ladybird* books. Subject matter of early readers a bit tedious and illustrations, though colourful and well produced, represent characters a little remote from most ordinary children. Grading rather steep. But the books are attractive and there is a very good range of supplementary material.

Let's Learn to Read (Blackie, 1960)
Mixed method—emphasis on look-and-say, but also some phonics.
Illustrations a bit dull. Subject matter more relevant to children than
some, and the interest of this helps the illustrations along.

Pilot (E. J. Arnold, 1953)
Emphasis on interest, particularly noticeable in later books for good
readers. An excellent scheme for this purpose. Strongly sentence
method, difficult to modify for anything else. Presents some difficulties
for slow readers. Good illustrations.

Royal Road (Chatto & Windus, 1956–70)
Look-and-say at first, but the objective is the phonic word approach
and the two are extremely well integrated. Based on very careful examination of how children learn to read (Daniels and Diack). Subject
matter in early books unexciting and language sometimes remote. New
edition more colourful and attractively presented. Some supplementary
material.

Through the Rainbow (Schofield & Sims, 1965)
Mainly sentence method, with phonics later. An easy style. Subject
matter more related to the young child's experiences than many schemes.
First books illustrated by photographs and concerned with families on
a housing estate. Phonics on the whole well planned, but with rather
a slow progression and introduced later than in many schemes. An
advantage is that the books are short, and the print in the early books
is larger than in most schemes.

Time for Reading (Ginn, 1967)
Strongly weighted towards look-and-say (sentence method in earlier
books). Adaptable to language-experience approach and lends itself
well to supplementary classroom activities. This helps to overcome the
disadvantage of grading which is too steep. Subject matter very appropriate to interests of young children. Delightful illustrations. Attractive introductory picture book and teacher's book of stories and poems.
Excellent range of supplementary material.

Note: Dr Elizabeth Goodacre's booklet *Hearing Children Read*, which
has been quoted in the text, includes a very full list of reading schemes
and other materials and gives a good deal of information about them.
It is obtainable from the Centre for the Teaching of Reading, 29
Eastern Avenue, Reading, Berks., RG1 5RU.

Appendix C

Key words[1]

The most used words in English, applied to the vocabulary of the average person (sectionalised according to frequency of use)

a and he I in is it of that the to was

all as at be but are for had have him his not
on one said so they we with you

about an back been before big by call came can
come could did do down first from get go has her
here if into just like little lock made make me
more much must my no new now off only or our
over other out right see she some their them then
there this two up want well went who were what
when where which will your old

The next hundred most common words

after again always am another any ask away bad
because best bird black blue boy bring day dog
don't eat every far fast father fell find five fly
four found gave girl give going good got green
hand head help home house how jump keep know
last left let live long man many may men mother
Mr never next once open own play put ran read
red room round run sat saw say school should sing
sit soon stop take tell than these thing think three
time too tree under us very walk white why wish
work would year

[1] From J. McNally and W. Murray, *Key Words to Literacy* (London, Schoolmaster Publishing Co., 1962).

Appendix D

The order of sounds

There does not appear to be general agreement on the order in which it is best to introduce sounds to children. Moreover, such information as is available applies to the order of sounds for phonic instruction in the teaching of reading. It would be very helpful if we knew something about the order in which we should introduce sounds for children when they learn to write, because this is not necessarily the same as that which applies when they are learning to read. However, in the absence of evidence on this point, and bearing in mind that there is some lack of agreement concerning the practice recommended for the teaching of reading, the information given below may serve as a guide to the teacher though she should not regard it as a gospel.

No attempt has been made to include every possible combination of sounds with which the child may concern himself. Such a list would be too complex and too full of qualifications to be of practical value. Only the main outline steps are given.

Suggested order of sounds for the teaching of reading
(Common sense modification will be needed for the teaching of writing.)
1. The common single consonants: among these are *b, d, m, n. o, t, g*, but this is not a 'scientific' list to which the teacher should rigidly adhere. The less common consonant sounds should be introduced in due course as they arise. At an appropriate time attention should be drawn to the fact that *c* and *g* each have two sounds.
2. The short vowel sounds.
3. Plurals with *s*.
4. The three common consonant digraphs which cannot be separated: *ch, sh, th* (*th* has two sounds, as in *th*is and *th*in; of the two, the sound as in *th*is is by far the more commonly used). *Wh* is also sometimes regarded as an inseparable consonant digraph. This applies in Scottish speech but not in English since the *h* is rarely sounded.
5. The common consonant digraphs which are not inseparable but which in practice are usefully treated as blends: there are ten of these: *br, cr, fr, gr, tr, bl, cl, fl, sl, st*. It would be better to begin with one or two and introduce them gradually.
6. The suffixes *ing* and *ed*; the double consonant *ck*.
7. The long vowel sounds and the use of the silent terminal *e*.
8. The suffixes *er, ly* and *y* (as in *baby*).

9. The common vowel combinations: *ee, oo* (both sounds, as in *look* and *food*), *ea, oa, ai, ay*.
10. The simple three-consonant combinations: *scr, spr, str, spl, thr*.
11. The more difficult vowel combinations: *ie, oi, oy, ou, ow, ew*.
12. Vowel sounds with *r*: *ar, er* (taught only as a suffix until now), *ir, or, ur*.
13. The 'rule' for soft *c* and *g*—usually before *e, i* and *y*.

This is probably as far as phonic training is likely to go in the First School, and clearly the later steps will apply only to the most advanced children.

Note: The teacher should not feel obliged to introduce every sound in any one of the categories given before beginning with anything in the next category. Common sense in the practical situation will be her best guide.

Bibliography

Artley, A. Sterl, 'The Teacher Variable in the Teaching of Reading', *The Reading Teacher*, vol. 23, no. 3 (Dec. 1969)

Burt, Cyril, *The Backward Child* (4th edn.) (London, University of London Press, 1958)

Cane, Brian and Smithers, Jane in Chanan, Gabriel (ed.), *The Roots of Reading* (Slough, National Foundation for Educational Research, 1971)

Cass, Joan E., *Literature and the Young Child* (London, Longman, 1967)

Central Advisory Council for Education (England), *Children and their Primary Schools* (Plowden Report) (London, H.M.S.O., 1967)

Chall, Jeanne, *Learning to Read: The Great Debate* (New York, McGraw Hill, 1967)

Clark, Margaret M., *Reading Difficulties in Schools* (Harmondsworth, Penguin Education, 1970)

Clegg, A. B. (ed.), *The Excitement of Writing* (London, Chatto & Windus, 1967)

Clift, P. S., 'The organisation of remedial teaching of children with reading difficulties', *Reading*, vol. I, no. 1 (March 1967)

Crouch, Boyd (ed.), *Overcoming Learning Difficulties* (London, Ernest Benn, 1972)

Daniels, J. C. and Diack, Hunter, *Progress in Reading in the Infant School* (Nottingham, University of Nottingham Institute of Education, 1960)

Daniels, J. C. (ed.), *Reading: Problems and Perspectives* (United Kingdom Reading Association, 1970)

Dean, Joan, *Reading, Writing and Talking* (London, Black, 1968)

Dearden, R. F., *The Philosophy of Primary Education* (London, Routledge & Kegan Paul, 1968)

Diack, Hunter, *In Spite of the Alphabet* (London, Chatto & Windus, 1965)

Downing, J. A., *The i.t.a. Reading Experiment* (London, Evans, 1964)

Downing, John and Thackray, D. V., *Reading Readiness* (London, University of London Press, 1971)

Eyre, Wallace, *Let's Imagine* Series, Book I (Oxford, Blackwell, 1966–7)

Fraser, H. and O'Donnell, W. R. (eds.), *Applied Linguistics and the Teaching of English* (London, Longman, 1969)

Fries, C. C., *Linguistics and Reading* (New York, Holt, Rinehart & Winston, 1962)

Gardner, Keith, 'The prevention of reading failure', *Reading*, vol. II, no. 3 (Dec. 1968); *Towards Literacy* (Oxford, Blackwell, 1965)

Gattegno, C., *Words in Colour: Background and Principles, Words in Colour: Teacher's Guide* (Reading, Educational Explorers Ltd, 1962)

Goodacre, Elizabeth J., *Reading in Infant Classes* (Slough, National Foundation for Educational Research, 1967); *Children and Learning to Read* (London, Routledge & Kegan Paul, 1971); *Hearing Children Read* (Reading, The Centre for Teaching Reading, 1972)

Hughes, John M., *Aids to Reading* (London, Evans, 1970)

Lane, S. M. and Kemp, M., *An Approach to Creative Writing in the Primary School* (London & Glasgow, Blackie, 1967)

Latham, Dorothy, *Six Reading Schemes: Their Emphases and Their Interchangeability* (Cambridge, University of Cambridge Institute of Education, 1971)

Lefevre, C. A., *Linguistics and the Teaching of Reading* (New York, McGraw Hill, 1964)

Lewis, M. M., *Language and the Child* (London, N.F.E.R., 1969)

Lovell, K., *Educational Psychology and Children* (5th edn.) (London, University of London Press, 1962)

Mackay, David, Thompson, Brian and Schaub, Pamela, *Breakthrough to Literacy: Teacher's Manual* (London, Longman for the Schools Council, 1970)

Mackay, David and Thompson, Brian, *The Initial Teaching of Reading and Writing: some notes towards a Theory of Literacy*, Programme in Linguistics and English Teaching, Paper no. 3 (1968, Communication Research Centre, University College, London and Longman)

McNally, J. and Murray, W., *Key Words to Literacy* (London, Schoolmaster Publishing Co., 1962)

Mellor, E., *Education Through Experience in the Infant School Years* (Oxford, Blackwell, 1950)

Merritt, John (ed.), *Reading and the Curriculum* (London, Ward Lock Educational for U.K.R.A., 1971)

Morris, Joyce, *Standards and Progress in Reading* (London, N.F.E.R., 1966)

Moyle, Donald, *The Teaching of Reading* (2nd edn.) (London, Ward Lock Educational, 1970)

Moyle, Donald and Louise M., *Modern Innovations in the Teaching of Reading* (London, University of London Press for U.K.R.A., 1971)

Peters, Margaret L., *Spelling: Caught or Taught?* (London, Routledge & Kegan Paul, 1967); *Success in Spelling* (Cambridge, University of Cambridge Institute of Education, 1970); *Trends in Reading Schemes* (Cambridge, University of Cambridge Institute of Education, 1971)

Reid, Jessie F., 'Talking, thinking and learning', *Reading*, vol. I, no. 1 (March 1967)

Roberts, Geoffrey R., *Reading in Primary Schools* (London, Routledge & Kegan Paul, 1969); 'Towards a Linguistic Approach to Reading', *Reading*, vol. I, no. 1 (March 1967)

Sabaroff, Rose E., 'Improving achievement in beginning reading', *The Reading Teacher*, vol. 23, no. 6 (March 1970)

Schonell, Fred J., *Backwardness in the Basic Subjects* (4th edn.) (Edinburgh, Oliver & Boyd, 1948); *The Psychology and Teaching of Reading* (4th edn.) (Edinburgh, Oliver & Boyd, 1961)

Southgate, Vera and Roberts, G. R., *Reading—Which Approach?* (London, University of London Press, 1970)

Start, K. B. and Wells, B. K., *The Trend of Reading Standards* (N.F.E.R., 1972)

Stones, E., *An Introduction to Educational Psychology* (London, Methuen, 1966)

Stott, D. H., *Roads to Literacy* (Glasgow, Holmes, 1964)

Tansley, A. E., *Reading and Remedial Reading* (London, Routledge & Kegan Paul, 1967)

Taylor, Joy, *Organising and Integrating the Infant Day* (London, Allen & Unwin, 1971)

Vernon, M. D., *Reading and Its Difficulties* (London, Cambridge University Press, 1971)

Warburton, F. W. and Southgate, V., *i.t.a.: An Independent Evaluation* (London, Chambers and Edinburgh, Murray, 1969)

Watts, A. F., *The Language and Mental Development of Children* (London, Harrap, 1944)

Webb, Lesley, *Children with Special Needs in the Infants' School* (London, Collins, Fontana Books, 1969)

Wilkinson, Andrew, *The Foundations of Language* (London, Oxford University Press, 1971)

Yates, Alfred, 'The Teaching of Reading from the Researcher's Point of View', *Child Education* (Autumn Quarterly 1954)

Index